MznLnx

Missing Links Exam Preps

Exam Prep for

Entrepreneurial Finance

Smith & Smith, 2nd Edition

The MznLnx Exam Prep is your link from the texbook and lecture to your exams.
The MznLnx Exam Preps are unauthorized and comprehensive reviews of your textbooks.

All material provided by MznLnx and Rico Publications (c) 2010
Textbook publishers and textbook authors do not particpate in or contribute to these reviews.

MznLnx

Rico
Publications

Exam Prep for Entrepreneurial Finance
2nd Edition
Smith & Smith

Publisher: Raymond Houge
Assistant Editor: Michael Rouger
Text and Cover Designer: Lisa Buckner
Marketing Manager: Sara Swagger
Project Manager, Editorial Production: Jerry Emerson
Art Director: Vernon Lowerui

Product Manager: Dave Mason
Editorial Assitant: Rachel Guzmanji
Pedagogy: Debra Long
Cover Image: Jim Reed/Getty Images
Text and Cover Printer: City Printing, Inc.
Compositor: Media Mix, Inc.

(c) 2010 Rico Publications
ALL RIGHTS RESERVED. No part of this work
covered by the copyright may be reproduced or
used in any form or by an means--graphic, electronic,
or mechanical, including photocopying, recording,
taping, Web distribution, information storage, and
retrieval systems, or in any other manner--without the
written permission of the publisher.

Printed in the United States
ISBN:

For more information about our products, contact us at:

Dave.Mason@RicoPublications.com

For permission to use material from this text or

product, submit a request online to:

Dave.Mason@RicoPublications.com

Contents

CHAPTER 1
Introduction — 1

CHAPTER 2
An Overview of New Venture Financing — 10

CHAPTER 3
The Business Plan — 21

CHAPTER 4
New Venture Strategy — 29

CHAPTER 5
Developing Business Strategy Using Simulation — 36

CHAPTER 6
Methods of Financial Forecasting — 40

CHAPTER 7
Assessing Financial Needs — 51

CHAPTER 8
The Framework of New Venture Valuation — 59

CHAPTER 9
Valuation in Practice: The Investor`s Perspective — 66

CHAPTER 10
Valuation: The Entrepreneur`s Perspective — 75

CHAPTER 11
Financial Contracting with Symmetric Information — 82

CHAPTER 12
Dealing with Information and Incentive Problems — 89

CHAPTER 13
Financial Contracting — 98

CHAPTER 14
Venture Capital — 104

CHAPTER 15
Harvesting — 116

ANSWER KEY — 129

TO THE STUDENT

COMPREHENSIVE

The *MznLnx* Exam Prep series is designed to help you pass your exams. Editors at MznLnx review your textbooks and then prepare these practice exams to help you master the textbook material. Unlike study guides, workbooks, and practice tests provided by the texbook publisher and textbook authors, *MznLnx* gives you **all** of the material in each chapter in exam form, not just samples, so you can be sure to nail your exam.

MECHANICAL

The MznLnx Exam Prep series creates exams that will help you learn the subject matter as well as test you on your understanding. Each question is designed to help you master the concept. Just working through the exams, you gain an understanding of the subject--its a simple mechanical process that produces success.

INTEGRATED STUDY GUIDE AND REVIEW

MznLnx is not just a set of exams designed to test you, its also a comprehensive review of the subject content. Each exam question is also a review of the concept, making sure that you will get the answer correct without having to go to other sources of material. You learn as you go! Its the easiest way to pass an exam.

HUMOR

Studying can be tedious and dry. MznLnx's instructional design includes moderate humor within the exam questions on occassion, to break the tedium and revitalize the brain

Chapter 1. Introduction

a. Sliding scale fees
c. Marginal cost
b. Fixed costs
d. Cost

13. The _____ is an expected return that the provider of capital plans to earn on their investment.

Capital (money) used for funding a business should earn returns for the capital providers who risk their capital. For an investment to be worthwhile, the expected return on capital must be greater than the _____.

a. 4-4-5 Calendar
c. Capital intensity
b. Weighted average cost of capital
d. Cost of capital

14. In finance, _____ is the process of estimating the potential market value of a financial asset or liability. they can be done on assets (for example, investments in marketable securities such as stocks, options, business enterprises, or intangible assets such as patents and trademarks) or on liabilities (e.g., Bonds issued by a company.) _____s are required in many contexts including investment analysis, capital budgeting, merger and acquisition transactions, financial reporting, taxable events to determine the proper tax liability, and in litigation.

a. Procter ' Gamble
c. Margin
b. Share
d. Valuation

15. The term _____ refers to three closely related concepts:

- The _____ model is a mathematical model of the market for an equity, in which the equity's price is a stochastic process.
- The _____ PDE is a partial differential equation which (in the model) must be satisfied by the price of a derivative on the equity.
- The _____ formula is the result obtained by solving the _____ PDE for a European call option.

Fischer Black and Myron Scholes first articulated the _____ formula in their 1973 paper, 'The Pricing of Options and Corporate Liabilities.' The foundation for their research relied on work developed by scholars such as Jack L. Treynor, Paul Samuelson, A. James Boness, Sheen T. Kassouf, and Edward O. Thorp. The fundamental insight of _____ is that the option is implicitly priced if the stock is traded.

Robert C. Merton was the first to publish a paper expanding the mathematical understanding of the options pricing model and coined the term '_____' options pricing model.

a. Perpetuity
c. Stochastic volatility
b. Black-Scholes
d. Modified Internal Rate of Return

16. _____ can be regarded as an outcome of mental processes (cognitive process) leading to the selection of a course of action among several alternatives. Every _____ process produces a final choice. The output can be an action or an opinion of choice.

a. 4-4-5 Calendar
c. 7-Eleven
b. Decision making
d. 529 plan

Chapter 1. Introduction

17. _____ is a mathematical science pertaining to the collection, analysis, interpretation or explanation, and presentation of data. It also provides tools for prediction and forecasting based on data. It is applicable to a wide variety of academic disciplines, from the natural and social sciences to the humanities, government and business.
   a. Mean
   b. Covariance
   c. Sample size
   d. Statistics

18. A sole _____, or simply _____ is a type of business entity which legally has no separate existence from its owner. Hence, the limitations of liability enjoyed by a corporation and limited liability partnerships do not apply to sole proprietors. All debts of the business are debts of the owner.
   a. Just-in-time
   b. Proprietorship
   c. Product life cycle
   d. Free cash flow

19. _____ is used to assign the available resources in an economic way. It is part of resource management.

In strategic planning, a _____ decision is a plan for using available resources, for example human resources, especially in the near term, to achieve goals for the future.

   a. 4-4-5 Calendar
   b. 7-Eleven
   c. Resource allocation
   d. 529 plan

20. In business and accounting, _____s are everything of value that is owned by a person or company. The balance sheet of a firm records the monetary value of the _____s owned by the firm. The two major _____ classes are tangible _____s and intangible _____s.
   a. Asset
   b. Income
   c. EBITDA
   d. Accounts payable

21. The term _____ has three unrelated technical definitions, and is also used in a variety of non-technical ways.

   - In financial economics, it refers to any asset used to make money, as opposed to assets used for personal enjoyment or consumption. This is an important distinction because two people can disagree sharply about the value of personal assets, one person might think a sports car is more valuable than a pickup truck, another person might have the opposite taste. But if an asset is held for the purpose of making money, taste has nothing to do with it, only differences of opinion about how much money the asset will produce. With the further assumption that people agree on the probability distribution of future cash flows, it is possible to have an objective _____ pricing model. Even without the assumption of agreement, it is possible to set rational limits on _____ value.
   - In governmental accounting, it is defined as any asset used in operations with an initial useful life extending beyond one reporting period. Generally, government managers have a 'stewardship' duty to maintain _____s under their control. See International Public Sector Accounting Standards for details.
   - In US tax accounting, it is defined as any property other than a list of exceptions. The main exceptions are anything held for sale, and any real estate or depreciable property used in business. Almost everything you own and use for personal purposes, pleasure or investment is a _____. If something is a _____ for tax purposes, gains or losses on sale or disposition are capital gains or capital losses. For individuals, however, capital losses on property held for personal use are generally not deductible. See the IRS publication Tax Facts about Capital Gains and Losses for details.

Chapter 1. Introduction

A well-known financial accounting textbook advises that the term be avoided except in tax accounting because it is used in so many different senses, not all of them well-defined. For example it is often used as a synonym for fixed assets or for investments in securities.

A common non-technical usage occurs when people ask that employees or the environment or something else be treated as a _____.

- a. Settlement date
- b. Capital Asset
- c. Solvency
- d. Political risk

22. In finance, the _____ is used to determine a theoretically appropriate required rate of return of an asset, if that asset is to be added to an already well-diversified portfolio, given that asset's non-diversifiable risk. The model takes into account the asset's sensitivity to non-diversifiable risk (also known as systemic risk or market risk), often represented by the quantity beta (β) in the financial industry, as well as the expected return of the market and the expected return of a theoretical risk-free asset.

The model was introduced by Jack Treynor (1961, 1962), William Sharpe (1964), John Lintner (1965a,b) and Jan Mossin (1966) independently, building on the earlier work of Harry Markowitz on diversification and modern portfolio theory.

- a. Random walk hypothesis
- b. Hull-White model
- c. Cox-Ingersoll-Ross model
- d. Capital Asset Pricing Model

23. A '_____' is a 'Charge' that is paid to obtain the right to delay a payment. Essentially, the payer purchases the right to make a given payment in the future instead of in the Present. The '_____', or 'Charge' that must be paid to delay the payment, is simply the difference between what the payment amount would be if it were paid in the present and what the payment amount would be paid if it were paid in the future.
- a. Risk modeling
- b. Value at risk
- c. Discount
- d. Risk aversion

24. The _____ is an interest rate a central bank charges depository institutions that borrow reserves from it.

The term _____ has two meanings:

- the same as interest rate; the term 'discount' does not refer to the meaning of the word, but to the purpose of using the quantity, such as computations of present value, e.g. net present value / discounted cash flow

- the annual effective _____, which is the annual interest divided by the capital including that interest; this rate is lower than the interest rate; it corresponds to using the value after a year as the nominal value, and seeing the initial value as the nominal value minus a discount; it is used for Treasury Bills and similar financial instruments

The annual effective _____ is the annual interest divided by the capital including that interest, which is the interest rate divided by 100% plus the interest rate. It is the annual discount factor to be applied to the future cash flow, to find the discount, subtracted from a future value to find the value one year earlier.

For example, suppose there is a government bond that sells for $95 and pays $100 in a year's time.

    a. Discount Rate
    b. Fisher equation
    c. Black-Scholes
    d. Stochastic volatility

25. _____ in finance is a risk management technique, related to hedging, that mixes a wide variety of investments within a portfolio. Because the fluctuations of a single security have less impact on a diverse portfolio, _____ minimizes the risk from any one investment.

A simple example of _____ is the following: On a particular island the entire economy consists of two companies: one that sells umbrellas and another that sells sunscreen.

    a. 7-Eleven
    b. 529 plan
    c. 4-4-5 Calendar
    d. Diversification

26. _____ are made by investors and investment managers.

Investors commonly perform investment analysis by making use of fundamental analysis, technical analysis and gut feel.

_____ are often supported by decision tools.

    a. Asset allocation
    b. Investment performance
    c. Investment decisions
    d. Investing online

27. _____ or net present worth (NPW) is defined as the total present value (PV) of a time series of cash flows. It is a standard method for using the time value of money to appraise long-term projects. Used for capital budgeting, and widely throughout economics, it measures the excess or shortfall of cash flows, in present value terms, once financing charges are met.

    a. Tax shield
    b. Net present value
    c. Negative gearing
    d. Present value of costs

28. _____ is the value on a given date of a future payment or series of future payments, discounted to reflect the time value of money and other factors such as investment risk. _____ calculations are widely used in business and economics to provide a means to compare cash flows at different times on a meaningful 'like to like' basis.

The most commonly applied model of the time value of money is compound interest.

a. Negative gearing
b. Present value of benefits
c. Net present value
d. Present value

29. A _____ is an exchange of promises between two or more parties to do an act which is enforceable in a court of law. It is where an unqualified offer meets a qualified acceptance and the parties reach Consensus ad Idem. The parties must have the necessary capacity to _____ and the _____ must not be either trifling, indeterminate, impossible or illegal.
   a. 529 plan
   b. 4-4-5 Calendar
   c. Contract
   d. 7-Eleven

30. In accounting, _____ refers to the portion of net income which is retained by the corporation rather than distributed to its owners as dividends. Similarly, if the corporation makes a loss, then that loss is retained and called variously retained losses, accumulated losses or accumulated deficit. _____ and losses are cumulative from year to year with losses offsetting earnings.
   a. Generally Accepted Accounting Principles
   b. Matching principle
   c. Historical cost
   d. Retained earnings

31. _____ is the balance of the amounts of cash being received and paid by a business during a defined period of time, sometimes tied to a specific project. Measurement of _____ can be used

- to evaluate the state or performance of a business or project.
- to determine problems with liquidity. Being profitable does not necessarily mean being liquid. A company can fail because of a shortage of cash, even while profitable.
- to generate project rate of returns. The time of _____s into and out of projects are used as inputs to financial models such as internal rate of return, and net present value.
- to examine income or growth of a business when it is believed that accrual accounting concepts do not represent economic realities. Alternately, _____ can be used to 'validate' the net income generated by accrual accounting.

_____ as a generic term may be used differently depending on context, and certain _____ definitions may be adapted by analysts and users for their own uses. Common terms include operating _____ and free _____.

_____s can be classified into:

1. Operational _____s: Cash received or expended as a result of the company's core business activities.
2. Investment _____s: Cash received or expended through capital expenditure, investments or acquisitions.
3. Financing _____s: Cash received or expended as a result of financial activities, such as interests and dividends.

All three together - the net _____ - are necessary to reconcile the beginning cash balance to the ending cash balance. Loan draw downs or equity injections, that is just shifting of capital but no expenditure as such, are not considered in the net _____.

8 *Chapter 1. Introduction*

    a. Real option
    b. Shareholder value
    c. Corporate finance
    d. Cash flow

32. A _____ is a payment made by a corporation to its shareholder members. When a corporation earns a profit or surplus, that money can be put to two uses: it can either be re-invested in the business (called retained earnings), or it can be paid to the shareholders as a _____. Many corporations retain a portion of their earnings and pay the remainder as a _____.

    a. Dividend puzzle
    b. Special dividend
    c. Dividend yield
    d. Dividend

33. In corporate finance, _____ is a cash flow available for distribution among all the security holders of a company. They include equity holders, debt holders, preferred stock holders, convertible security holders, and so on.

Note that the first three lines above are calculated for you on the standard Statement of Cash Flows.

    a. Free cash flow
    b. Funding
    c. Safety stock
    d. Forfaiting

34. In the theory of capital structure, _____ is the phrase used to describe funds that firms obtain from outside of the firm. It is contrasted to internal financing which consists mainly of profits retained by the firm for investment. There are many kinds of _____.

    a. Ownership equity
    b. Adjustment
    c. Asset-backed commercial paper
    d. External financing

35. _____ are legal property rights over creations of the mind, both artistic and commercial, and the corresponding fields of law. Under _____ law, owners are granted certain exclusive rights to a variety of intangible assets, such as musical, literary, and artistic works; ideas, discoveries and inventions; and words, phrases, symbols, and designs. Common types of _____ include copyrights, trademarks, patents, industrial design rights and trade secrets.

    a. AAB
    b. ABN Amro
    c. A Random Walk Down Wall Street
    d. Intellectual property

36. The phrase _____ refers to the aspect of corporate strategy, corporate finance and management dealing with the buying, selling and combining of different companies that can aid, finance, or help a growing company in a given industry grow rapidly without having to create another business entity.

An acquisition, also known as a takeover, is the buying of one company (the 'target') by another. An acquisition may be friendly or hostile.

    a. Mergers and acquisitions
    b. 4-4-5 Calendar
    c. 529 plan
    d. 7-Eleven

37. A _____ is a type of business entity in which partners (owners) share with each other the profits or losses of the business undertaking in which all have invested. _____s are often favored over corporations for taxation purposes, as the _____ structure does not generally incur a tax on profits before it is distributed to the partners (i.e. there is no dividend tax levied.) However, depending on the _____ structure and the jurisdiction in which it operates, owners of a _____ may be exposed to greater personal liability than they would as shareholders of a corporation.

a. Fiduciary
b. National Securities Markets Improvement Act of 1996
c. Clayton Antitrust Act
d. Partnership

38. _____ is a voluntary contract between two or among more than two persons to place their capital, labor, and skills, and corporation in business with the understanding that there will be a sharing of the profits and losses between/among partners. Outside of North America, it is normally referred to simply as a partnership agreement.
   a. Express warranty
   b. Economies of scale
   c. Economic depreciation
   d. Articles of Partnership

39. In finance, _____, also known as return on investment is the ratio of money gained or lost on an investment relative to the amount of money invested. The amount of money gained or lost may be referred to as interest, profit/loss, gain/loss, or net income/loss. The money invested may be referred to as the asset, capital, principal, or the cost basis of the investment.
   a. Composiition of Creditors
   b. Doctrine of the Proper Law
   c. Stock or scrip dividends
   d. Rate of return

Chapter 2. An Overview of New Venture Financing

1. _____ is a type of private equity capital typically provided to early-stage, high-potential, growth companies in the interest of generating a return through an eventual realization event such as an IPO or trade sale of the company. _____ investments are generally made as cash in exchange for shares in the invested company. It is typical for _____ investors to identify and back companies in high technology industries such as biotechnology and ICT.

   a. Treasury Inflation-Protected Securities
   b. Venture Capital
   c. Tail risk
   d. Probability distribution

2. _____ or financing is to provide capital (funds), which means money for a project, a person, a business or any other private or public institutions.

   Those funds can be allocated for either short term or long term purposes. The health fund is a new way of _____ private healthcare centers.

   a. Product life cycle
   b. Synthetic CDO
   c. Proxy fight
   d. Funding

3. A '_____' is a 'Charge' that is paid to obtain the right to delay a payment. Essentially, the payer purchases the right to make a given payment in the future instead of in the Present. The '_____', or 'Charge' that must be paid to delay the payment, is simply the difference between what the payment amount would be if it were paid in the present and what the payment amount would be paid if it were paid in the future.

   a. Risk modeling
   b. Risk aversion
   c. Value at risk
   d. Discount

4. The _____ is an interest rate a central bank charges depository institutions that borrow reserves from it.

   The term _____ has two meanings:

   - the same as interest rate; the term 'discount' does not refer to the meaning of the word, but to the purpose of using the quantity, such as computations of present value, e.g. net present value / discounted cash flow

   - the annual effective _____, which is the annual interest divided by the capital including that interest; this rate is lower than the interest rate; it corresponds to using the value after a year as the nominal value, and seeing the initial value as the nominal value minus a discount; it is used for Treasury Bills and similar financial instruments

   The annual effective _____ is the annual interest divided by the capital including that interest, which is the interest rate divided by 100% plus the interest rate. It is the annual discount factor to be applied to the future cash flow, to find the discount, subtracted from a future value to find the value one year earlier.

   For example, suppose there is a government bond that sells for $95 and pays $100 in a year's time.

   a. Black-Scholes
   b. Fisher equation
   c. Stochastic volatility
   d. Discount Rate

5. An _____ is a company whose main business is holding securities of other companies purely for investment purposes. The _____ invests money on behalf of its shareholders who in turn share in the profits and losses.

Chapter 2. An Overview of New Venture Financing

a. Unit investment trust
b. A Random Walk Down Wall Street
c. AAB
d. Investment company

6. An _____ is a contract written by a seller that conveys to the buyer the right -- but not the obligation -- to buy (in the case of a call _____) or to sell (in the case of a put _____) a particular asset, such as a piece of property such as, among others, a futures contract. In return for granting the _____, the seller collects a payment (the premium) from the buyer.

For example, buying a call _____ provides the right to buy a specified quantity of a security at a set strike price at some time on or before expiration, while buying a put _____ provides the right to sell.

a. Amortization
b. AT'T Mobility LLC
c. Annuity
d. Option

7. The _____ is the market for securities, where companies and governments can raise longterm funds. The _____ includes the stock market and the bond market. Financial regulators, such as the U.S. Securities and Exchange Commission, oversee the _____s in their designated countries to ensure that investors are protected against fraud.

a. Delta neutral
b. Spot rate
c. Capital market
d. Forward market

8. A _____ is an exchange of promises between two or more parties to do an act which is enforceable in a court of law. It is where an unqualified offer meets a qualified acceptance and the parties reach Consensus ad Idem. The parties must have the necessary capacity to _____ and the _____ must not be either trifling, indeterminate, impossible or illegal.

a. 529 plan
b. 4-4-5 Calendar
c. 7-Eleven
d. Contract

9. In finance, a _____ is a security that entitles the holder to buy stock of the company that issued it at a specified price, which is usually higher than the stock price at time of issue.

_____s are frequently attached to bonds or preferred stock as a sweetener, allowing the issuer to pay lower interest rates or dividends. They can be used to enhance the yield of the bond, and make them more attractive to potential buyers.

a. Clearing house
b. Warrant
c. Clearing
d. Credit

10. In business and accounting, _____s are everything of value that is owned by a person or company. The balance sheet of a firm records the monetary value of the _____s owned by the firm. The two major _____ classes are tangible _____s and intangible _____s.

a. Asset
b. Income
c. Accounts payable
d. EBITDA

11. In finance, _____ is the process of estimating the potential market value of a financial asset or liability. they can be done on assets (for example, investments in marketable securities such as stocks, options, business enterprises, or intangible assets such as patents and trademarks) or on liabilities (e.g., Bonds issued by a company.) _____s are required in many contexts including investment analysis, capital budgeting, merger and acquisition transactions, financial reporting, taxable events to determine the proper tax liability, and in litigation.

    a. Share   b. Valuation
    c. Margin   d. Procter ' Gamble

12. The term _____ refers to three closely related concepts:

- The _____ model is a mathematical model of the market for an equity, in which the equity's price is a stochastic process.
- The _____ PDE is a partial differential equation which (in the model) must be satisfied by the price of a derivative on the equity.
- The _____ formula is the result obtained by solving the _____ PDE for a European call option.

Fischer Black and Myron Scholes first articulated the _____ formula in their 1973 paper, 'The Pricing of Options and Corporate Liabilities.' The foundation for their research relied on work developed by scholars such as Jack L. Treynor, Paul Samuelson, A. James Boness, Sheen T. Kassouf, and Edward O. Thorp. The fundamental insight of _____ is that the option is implicitly priced if the stock is traded.

Robert C. Merton was the first to publish a paper expanding the mathematical understanding of the options pricing model and coined the term '_____' options pricing model.

    a. Stochastic volatility   b. Modified Internal Rate of Return
    c. Perpetuity   d. Black-Scholes

13. A _____ is a corporation in the United States that, for Federal income tax purposes, is taxed under 26 U.S.C. § 11 and Subchapter C (26 U.S.C. § 11 and Subchapter C (26 U.S.C. § 301 et seq.) of Chapter 1 of the Internal Revenue Code. Most major companies (and many smaller companies) are treated as _____ for Federal income tax purposes.

The income of a _____ is taxed, whereas the income of an S corporation (with a few exceptions) is not taxed under the Federal income tax laws. The income, or loss, is applied, Pro Rata, to each Shareholder and appears on their tax return as Schedule E income/(loss).

    a. 529 plan   b. 4-4-5 Calendar
    c. 7-Eleven   d. C corporation

Chapter 2. An Overview of New Venture Financing 13

14. The term _____ has three unrelated technical definitions, and is also used in a variety of non-technical ways.

   - In financial economics, it refers to any asset used to make money, as opposed to assets used for personal enjoyment or consumption. This is an important distinction because two people can disagree sharply about the value of personal assets, one person might think a sports car is more valuable than a pickup truck, another person might have the opposite taste. But if an asset is held for the purpose of making money, taste has nothing to do with it, only differences of opinion about how much money the asset will produce. With the further assumption that people agree on the probability distribution of future cash flows, it is possible to have an objective _____ pricing model. Even without the assumption of agreement, it is possible to set rational limits on _____ value.
   - In governmental accounting, it is defined as any asset used in operations with an initial useful life extending beyond one reporting period. Generally, government managers have a 'stewardship' duty to maintain _____s under their control. See International Public Sector Accounting Standards for details.
   - In US tax accounting, it is defined as any property other than a list of exceptions. The main exceptions are anything held for sale, and any real estate or depreciable property used in business. Almost everything you own and use for personal purposes, pleasure or investment is a _____. If something is a _____ for tax purposes, gains or losses on sale or disposition are capital gains or capital losses. For individuals, however, capital losses on property held for personal use are generally not deductible. See the IRS publication Tax Facts about Capital Gains and Losses for details.

A well-known financial accounting textbook advises that the term be avoided except in tax accounting because it is used in so many different senses, not all of them well-defined. For example it is often used as a synonym for fixed assets or for investments in securities.

A common non-technical usage occurs when people ask that employees or the environment or something else be treated as a _____.

   a. Capital Asset
   b. Solvency
   c. Political risk
   d. Settlement date

15. In finance, the _____ is used to determine a theoretically appropriate required rate of return of an asset, if that asset is to be added to an already well-diversified portfolio, given that asset's non-diversifiable risk. The model takes into account the asset's sensitivity to non-diversifiable risk (also known as systemic risk or market risk), often represented by the quantity beta (β) in the financial industry, as well as the expected return of the market and the expected return of a theoretical risk-free asset.

The model was introduced by Jack Treynor (1961, 1962), William Sharpe (1964), John Lintner (1965a,b) and Jan Mossin (1966) independently, building on the earlier work of Harry Markowitz on diversification and modern portfolio theory.

   a. Random walk hypothesis
   b. Hull-White model
   c. Cox-Ingersoll-Ross model
   d. Capital Asset Pricing Model

16. An _____ is a corporation that makes a valid election to be taxed under Subchapter S of Chapter 1 of the Internal Revenue Code.

Chapter 2. An Overview of New Venture Financing

In general, _____s do not pay any income taxes. Instead, the corporation's income or losses are divided among and passed through to its shareholders.

   a. 4-4-5 Calendar   b. 529 plan
   c. 7-Eleven   d. S corporation

17. A _____ is a fungible, negotiable instrument representing financial value. They are broadly categorized into debt securities (such as banknotes, bonds and debentures), and equity securities; e.g., common stocks. The company or other entity issuing the _____ is called the issuer.
   a. Security   b. Tracking stock
   c. Book entry   d. Securities lending

18. The _____ is the guaranteed payoff at which a person is 'indifferent' between accepting the guaranteed payoff and a higher but uncertain payoff. (It is the amount of the higher payout minus the risk premium).
   a. 7-Eleven   b. 4-4-5 Calendar
   c. 529 plan   d. Certainty equivalent

19. The institution most often referenced by the word '_____' is a public or publicly traded _____, the shares of which are traded on a public stock exchange (e.g., the New York Stock Exchange or Nasdaq in the United States) where shares of stock of _____s are bought and sold by and to the general public. Most of the largest businesses in the world are publicly traded _____s. However, the majority of _____s are said to be closely held, privately held or close _____s, meaning that no ready market exists for the trading of shares.
   a. Federal Home Loan Mortgage Corporation   b. Depository Trust Company
   c. Protect   d. Corporation

20. In economics, business, and accounting, a _____ is the value of money that has been used up to produce something, and hence is not available for use anymore. In business, the _____ may be one of acquisition, in which case the amount of money expended to acquire it is counted as _____. In this case, money is the input that is gone in order to acquire the thing.
   a. Cost   b. Marginal cost
   c. Sliding scale fees   d. Fixed costs

21. The _____ is an expected return that the provider of capital plans to earn on their investment.

Capital (money) used for funding a business should earn returns for the capital providers who risk their capital. For an investment to be worthwhile, the expected return on capital must be greater than the _____.

   a. 4-4-5 Calendar   b. Capital intensity
   c. Weighted average cost of capital   d. Cost of capital

22. _____ are legal property rights over creations of the mind, both artistic and commercial, and the corresponding fields of law. Under _____ law, owners are granted certain exclusive rights to a variety of intangible assets, such as musical, literary, and artistic works; ideas, discoveries and inventions; and words, phrases, symbols, and designs. Common types of _____ include copyrights, trademarks, patents, industrial design rights and trade secrets.

Chapter 2. An Overview of New Venture Financing 15

a. ABN Amro
c. A Random Walk Down Wall Street
b. Intellectual property
d. AAB

23. A sole _____, or simply _____ is a type of business entity which legally has no separate existence from its owner. Hence, the limitations of liability enjoyed by a corporation and limited liability partnerships do not apply to sole proprietors. All debts of the business are debts of the owner.

a. Free cash flow
c. Proprietorship
b. Just-in-time
d. Product life cycle

24. _____ right are usage-based payments made by one party to another (the 'licensor') for ongoing use of an asset, sometimes an intellectual property (IP) right..

_____ can be determined as a percentage of gross or net sales derived from use of the asset or a fixed price per unit sold. but there are also other modes and metrics of compensation.

a. Due diligence
c. Celler-Kefauver Act
b. Financial Institutions Reform Recovery and Enforcement Act
d. Royalties

25. _____ is the price at which an asset would trade in a competitive Walrasian auction setting. _____ is often used interchangeably with open _____, fair value or fair _____, although these terms have distinct definitions in different standards, and may differ in some circumstances.

International Valuation Standards defines _____ as 'the estimated amount for which a property should exchange on the date of valuation between a willing buyer and a willing seller in an arm'e;s-length transaction after proper marketing wherein the parties had each acted knowledgeably, prudently, and without compulsion.'

_____ is a concept distinct from market price, which is 'e;the price at which one can transact'e;, while _____ is 'e;the true underlying value'e; according to theoretical standards.

a. Market value
c. Wrap account
b. Debt restructuring
d. T-Model

26. In business and finance, a _____ (also referred to as equity _____) of stock means a _____ of ownership in a corporation (company.) In the plural, stocks is often used as a synonym for _____s especially in the United States, but it is less commonly used that way outside of North America.

In the United Kingdom, South Africa, and Australia, stock can also refer to completely different financial instruments such as government bonds or, less commonly, to all kinds of marketable securities.

a. Margin
c. Bucket shop
b. Share
d. Procter ' Gamble

27. The _____ of 1974 (Pub.L. 93-406, 88 Stat. 829, enacted September 2, 1974) is an American federal statute that establishes minimum standards for pension plans in private industry and provides for extensive rules on the federal income tax effects of transactions associated with employee benefit plans.

a. Express warranty
c. Expedited Funds Availability Act
b. Articles of Partnership
d. Employee Retirement Income Security Act

28. _____, refers to consumption opportunity gained by an entity within a specified time frame, which is generally expressed in monetary terms. However, for households and individuals, '_____ is the sum of all the wages, salaries, profits, interests payments, rents and other forms of earnings received... in a given period of time.' For firms, _____ generally refers to net-profit: what remains of revenue after expenses have been subtracted.
   a. Income
   b. OIBDA
   c. Annual report
   d. Accrual

29. _____, in bookkeeping, refers to assets, liabilities, income, and expenses recorded on individual pages of the so called book of final entry or ledger. Changes in _____ value are made by chronologically posting debit (DR) and credit (CR) entries to its page. Examples of _____s are cash, _____s receivable, mortgages, loans, land and buildings, common stock, sales, services provided, wages, and payroll overhead.
   a. Option
   b. Alpha
   c. Accretion
   d. Account

30. _____ is one of a series of accounting transactions dealing with the billing of customers who owe money to a person, company or organization for goods and services that have been provided to the customer. In most business entities this is typically done by generating an invoice and mailing or electronically delivering it to the customer, who in turn must pay it within an established timeframe called credit or payment terms.

An example of a common payment term is Net 30, meaning payment is due in the amount of the invoice 30 days from the date of invoice.

   a. Accounts receivable
   b. Impaired asset
   c. Accounting methods
   d. Income

31. _____ is a method for constructing a (zero-coupon) fixed-income yield curve from the prices of a set of coupon-bearing products by forward substitution.

Using these zero-coupon products it becomes possible to derive par swap rates (forward and spot) for all maturities by making a few assumptions (including linear interpolation.) The term structure of spot returns is recovered from the bond yields by solving for them recursively, this iterative process is called the BootStrap Method.

   a. Bootstrapping
   b. Bullet loan
   c. Reserve requirement
   d. Probability of default

32. _____ is a method of financing, used to maintain liquidity while waiting for an anticipated and reasonably expected inflow of cash. _____ is commonly used when the cash flow from a sale of an asset is expected after the cash outlay for the purchase of an asset. For example, when selling a house, the owner may not receive the cash for 90 days, but has already purchased a new home and must pay for it in 30 days.
   a. Bridge financing
   b. Liquidation value
   c. Real estate investing
   d. Tenancy

Chapter 2. An Overview of New Venture Financing

33. A _____ occurs when a financial sponsor acquires a controlling interest in a company's equity and where a significant percentage of the purchase price is financed through leverage (borrowing.) The assets of the acquired company are used as collateral for the borrowed capital, sometimes with assets of the acquiring company. The bonds or other paper issued for _____s are commonly considered not to be investment grade because of the significant risks involved.

   a. Leverage
   b. Pension fund
   c. Limited partnership
   d. Leveraged buyout

34. In the theory of capital structure, _____ is the phrase used to describe funds that firms obtain from outside of the firm. It is contrasted to internal financing which consists mainly of profits retained by the firm for investment. There are many kinds of _____.

   a. Asset-backed commercial paper
   b. Adjustment
   c. Ownership equity
   d. External financing

35. A _____ is a pool of assets forming an independent legal entity that are bought with the contributions to a pension plan for the exclusive purpose of financing pension plan benefits.

   _____s are important shareholders of listed and private companies. They are especially important to the stock market where large institutional investors like the Ontario Teachers' Pension Plan dominate.

   a. Leveraged buyout
   b. Limited liability company
   c. Leverage
   d. Pension fund

36. An _____ or angel is an affluent individual who provides capital for a business start-up, usually in exchange for convertible debt or ownership equity. A small but increasing number of _____s organize themselves into angel groups or angel networks to share research and pool their investment capital.

   Angels typically invest their own funds, unlike venture capitalists, who manage the pooled money of others in a professionally-managed fund.

   a. AAB
   b. A Random Walk Down Wall Street
   c. ABN Amro
   d. Angel investor

37. _____ is the provision of resources (such as granting a loan) by one party to another party where that second party does not reimburse the first party immediately, thereby generating a debt, and instead arranges either to repay or return those resources (or material(s) of equal value) at a later date. The first party is called a creditor, also known as a lender, while the second party is called a debtor, also known as a borrower.

   Movements of financial capital are normally dependent on either _____ or equity transfers.

   a. Clearing house
   b. Credit
   c. Comparable
   d. Warrant

38. _____ is a financial transaction whereby a business sells its accounts receivable (i.e., invoices) at a discount. _____ differs from a bank loan in three main ways. First, the emphasis is on the value of the receivables (essentially a financial asset), not the firm's credit worthiness.

a. Credit card balance transfer
b. Factoring
c. Financial Literacy Month
d. Debt-for-equity swap

39. _____ is an organization's process of defining its strategy and making decisions on allocating its resources to pursue this strategy, including its capital and people. Various business analysis techniques can be used in _____, including SWOT analysis (Strengths, Weaknesses, Opportunities, and Threats) and PEST analysis (Political, Economic, Social, and Technological analysis) or STEER analysis involving Socio-cultural, Technological, Economic, Ecological, and Regulatory factors and EPISTEL (Environment, Political, Informatic, Social, Technological, Economic and Legal)

_____ is the formal consideration of an organization's future course. All _____ deals with at least one of three key questions:

1. 'What do we do?'
2. 'For whom do we do it?'
3. 'How do we excel?'

In business _____, the third question is better phrased 'How can we beat or avoid competition?'. (Bradford and Duncan, page 1.)

a. 529 plan
b. 4-4-5 Calendar
c. 7-Eleven
d. Strategic planning

40. _____ exists when one firm provides goods or services to a customer with an agreement to bill them later, or receive a shipment or service from a supplier under an agreement to pay them later. It can be viewed as an essential element of capitalization in an operating business because it can reduce the required capital investment to operate the business if it is managed properly. _____ is the largest use of capital for a majority of business to business (B2B) sellers in the United States and is a critical source of capital for a majority of all businesses.

a. 4-4-5 Calendar
b. Trade credit
c. Going concern
d. 529 plan

41. A _____ is a financial contract between two parties, the buyer and the seller of this type of option. Often it is simply labeled a 'call'. The buyer of the option has the right, but not the obligation to buy an agreed quantity of a particular commodity or financial instrument (the underlying instrument) from the seller of the option at a certain time (the expiration date) for a certain price (the strike price.)

a. Bear spread
b. Bull spread
c. Bear call spread
d. Call Option

42. A _____ is a decision support tool that uses a tree-like graph or model of decisions and their possible consequences, including chance event outcomes, resource costs, and utility. _____s are commonly used in operations research, specifically in decision analysis, to help identify a strategy most likely to reach a goal. Another use of _____s is as a descriptive means for calculating conditional probabilities.

a. Decision tree
b. 529 plan
c. 7-Eleven
d. 4-4-5 Calendar

Chapter 2. An Overview of New Venture Financing

43. In the United States, a _____ is an offering of securities that are not registered with the Securities and Exchange Commission (SEC.) Such offerings exploit an exemption offered by the Securities Act of 1933 that comes with several restrictions, including a prohibition against general solicitation. This exemption allows companies to avoid quarterly reporting requirements and many of the legal liabilities associated with the Sarbanes-Oxley Act.
   a. 529 plan
   b. Private placement
   c. 4-4-5 Calendar
   d. 7-Eleven

44. The U.S. _____ is an independent agency of the United States government which holds primary responsibility for enforcing the federal securities laws and regulating the securities industry, the nation's stock and options exchanges, and other electronic securities markets. The SEC was created by section 4 of the SEC of 1934 (now codified as 15 U.S.C. § 78d and commonly referred to as the 1934 Act.)
   a. Securities and Exchange Commission
   b. 7-Eleven
   c. 529 plan
   d. 4-4-5 Calendar

45. _____, is when a company issues common stock or shares to the public for the first time. They are often issued by smaller, younger companies seeking capital to expand, but can also be done by large privately-owned companies looking to become publicly traded.

   In an _____ the issuer may obtain the assistance of an underwriting firm, which helps it determine what type of security to issue (common or preferred), best offering price and time to bring it to market.

   a. Asian Financial Crisis
   b. Interest
   c. Insolvency
   d. Initial public offering

46. _____ are organizations which pool large sums of money and invest those sums in companies. They include banks, insurance companies, retirement or pension funds, hedge funds and mutual funds. Their role in the economy is to act as highly specialized investors on behalf of others.
   a. A Random Walk Down Wall Street
   b. ABN Amro
   c. Institutional investors
   d. AAB

47. _____ is that which is owed; usually referencing assets owed, but the term can cover other obligations. In the case of assets, _____ is a means of using future purchasing power in the present before a summation has been earned. Some companies and corporations use _____ as a part of their overall corporate finance strategy.
   a. Partial Payment
   b. Credit cycle
   c. Cross-collateralization
   d. Debt

48. _____ refers to the methods of practicing and using another person's business philosophy. The franchisor grants the independent operator the right to distribute its products, techniques, and trademarks for a percentage of gross monthly sales and a royalty fee. Various tangibles and intangibles such as national or international advertising, training, and other support services are commonly made available by the franchisor.
   a. 4-4-5 Calendar
   b. 529 plan
   c. 7-Eleven
   d. Franchising

Chapter 2. An Overview of New Venture Financing

49. _____ is a process by which a firm can obtain the use of a certain fixed assets for which it must pay a series of contractual, periodic, tax deductable payments. The lessee is the receiver of the services or the assets under the lease contract and the lessor is the owner of the assets. The relationship between the tenant and the landlord is called a tenancy, and can be for a fixed or an indefinite period of time (called the term of the lease).

   a. Quiet period   b. Royalties
   c. Leasing   d. Foreign Corrupt Practices Act

50. A _____, in its most general sense, is a solemn promise to engage in or refrain from a specified action.

More specifically, a _____, in contrast to a contract, is a one-way agreement whereby the _____er is the only party bound by the promise. A _____ may have conditions and prerequisites that qualify the undertaking, including the actions of second or third parties, but there is no inherent agreement by such other parties to fulfill those requirements.

   a. Covenant   b. Federal Trade Commission Act
   c. Clayton Antitrust Act   d. Partnership

51. The phrase _____ refers to the aspect of corporate strategy, corporate finance and management dealing with the buying, selling and combining of different companies that can aid, finance, or help a growing company in a given industry grow rapidly without having to create another business entity.

An acquisition, also known as a takeover, is the buying of one company (the 'target') by another. An acquisition may be friendly or hostile.

   a. 7-Eleven   b. 529 plan
   c. 4-4-5 Calendar   d. Mergers and acquisitions

52. In finance, a _____ is a type of bond that can be converted into shares of stock in the issuing company, usually at some pre-announced ratio. It is a hybrid security with debt- and equity-like features. Although it typically has a low coupon rate, the holder is compensated with the ability to convert the bond to common stock, usually at a substantial discount to the stock's market value.

   a. Bond fund   b. Gilts
   c. Corporate bond   d. Convertible bond

53. In financial accounting, _____s are precautions for which the amount or probability of occurrence are not known. Typical examples are _____s for warranty costs and _____ for taxes the term reserve is used instead of term _____; such a use, however, is inconsistent with the terminology suggested by International Accounting Standards Board.

   a. Money measurement concept   b. Provision
   c. Petty cash   d. Momentum Accounting and Triple-Entry Bookkeeping

Chapter 3. The Business Plan

1. The term _____ refers to three closely related concepts:

    - The _____ model is a mathematical model of the market for an equity, in which the equity's price is a stochastic process.
    - The _____ PDE is a partial differential equation which (in the model) must be satisfied by the price of a derivative on the equity.
    - The _____ formula is the result obtained by solving the _____ PDE for a European call option.

Fischer Black and Myron Scholes first articulated the _____ formula in their 1973 paper, 'The Pricing of Options and Corporate Liabilities.' The foundation for their research relied on work developed by scholars such as Jack L. Treynor, Paul Samuelson, A. James Boness, Sheen T. Kassouf, and Edward O. Thorp. The fundamental insight of _____ is that the option is implicitly priced if the stock is traded.

Robert C. Merton was the first to publish a paper expanding the mathematical understanding of the options pricing model and coined the term '_____' options pricing model.

   a. Stochastic volatility
   c. Black-Scholes
   b. Modified Internal Rate of Return
   d. Perpetuity

2. An _____ is a contract written by a seller that conveys to the buyer the right -- but not the obligation -- to buy (in the case of a call _____) or to sell (in the case of a put _____) a particular asset, such as a piece of property such as, among others, a futures contract. In return for granting the _____, the seller collects a payment (the premium) from the buyer.

For example, buying a call _____ provides the right to buy a specified quantity of a security at a set strike price at some time on or before expiration, while buying a put _____ provides the right to sell.

   a. Option
   c. AT'T Mobility LLC
   b. Amortization
   d. Annuity

3. _____ is a type of private equity capital typically provided to early-stage, high-potential, growth companies in the interest of generating a return through an eventual realization event such as an IPO or trade sale of the company. _____ investments are generally made as cash in exchange for shares in the invested company. It is typical for _____ investors to identify and back companies in high technology industries such as biotechnology and ICT.
   a. Tail risk
   c. Probability distribution
   b. Treasury Inflation-Protected Securities
   d. Venture Capital

4. A _____ is a corporation in the United States that, for Federal income tax purposes, is taxed under 26 U.S.C. Â§ 11 and Subchapter C (26 U.S.C. Â§ 11 and Subchapter C (26 U.S.C. Â§ 301 et seq.) of Chapter 1 of the Internal Revenue Code. Most major companies (and many smaller companies) are treated as _____ for Federal income tax purposes.

The income of a _____ is taxed, whereas the income of an S corporation (with a few exceptions) is not taxed under the Federal income tax laws. The income, or loss, is applied, Pro Rata, to each Shareholder and appears on their tax return as Schedule E income/(loss).

Chapter 3. The Business Plan

   a. 7-Eleven
   c. 4-4-5 Calendar
   b. C corporation
   d. 529 plan

5. An _____ is a corporation that makes a valid election to be taxed under Subchapter S of Chapter 1 of the Internal Revenue Code.

In general, _____s do not pay any income taxes. Instead, the corporation's income or losses are divided among and passed through to its shareholders.

   a. 529 plan
   c. 4-4-5 Calendar
   b. 7-Eleven
   d. S corporation

6. A _____ is a fungible, negotiable instrument representing financial value. They are broadly categorized into debt securities (such as banknotes, bonds and debentures), and equity securities; e.g., common stocks. The company or other entity issuing the _____ is called the issuer.
   - a. Book entry
   - b. Tracking stock
   - c. Securities lending
   - d. Security

7. The institution most often referenced by the word '_____' is a public or publicly traded _____, the shares of which are traded on a public stock exchange (e.g., the New York Stock Exchange or Nasdaq in the United States) where shares of stock of _____s are bought and sold by and to the general public. Most of the largest businesses in the world are publicly traded _____s. However, the majority of _____s are said to be closely held, privately held or close _____s, meaning that no ready market exists for the trading of shares.
   - a. Corporation
   - b. Depository Trust Company
   - c. Protect
   - d. Federal Home Loan Mortgage Corporation

8. In economics, business, and accounting, a _____ is the value of money that has been used up to produce something, and hence is not available for use anymore. In business, the _____ may be one of acquisition, in which case the amount of money expended to acquire it is counted as _____. In this case, money is the input that is gone in order to acquire the thing.
   - a. Marginal cost
   - b. Fixed costs
   - c. Sliding scale fees
   - d. Cost

9. The _____ is an expected return that the provider of capital plans to earn on their investment.

Capital (money) used for funding a business should earn returns for the capital providers who risk their capital. For an investment to be worthwhile, the expected return on capital must be greater than the _____.

   a. Weighted average cost of capital
   c. 4-4-5 Calendar
   b. Capital intensity
   d. Cost of capital

10. In finance, a _____ is a security that entitles the holder to buy stock of the company that issued it at a specified price, which is usually higher than the stock price at time of issue.

Chapter 3. The Business Plan

_____s are frequently attached to bonds or preferred stock as a sweetener, allowing the issuer to pay lower interest rates or dividends. They can be used to enhance the yield of the bond, and make them more attractive to potential buyers.

a. Clearing house
b. Credit
c. Clearing
d. Warrant

11. The _____ of 1974 (Pub.L. 93-406, 88 Stat. 829, enacted September 2, 1974) is an American federal statute that establishes minimum standards for pension plans in private industry and provides for extensive rules on the federal income tax effects of transactions associated with employee benefit plans.

a. Express warranty
b. Expedited Funds Availability Act
c. Articles of Partnership
d. Employee Retirement Income Security Act

12. _____, refers to consumption opportunity gained by an entity within a specified time frame, which is generally expressed in monetary terms. However, for households and individuals, '_____ is the sum of all the wages, salaries, profits, interests payments, rents and other forms of earnings received... in a given period of time.' For firms, _____ generally refers to net-profit: what remains of revenue after expenses have been subtracted.

a. Annual report
b. Income
c. OIBDA
d. Accrual

13. _____ can be regarded as an outcome of mental processes (cognitive process) leading to the selection of a course of action among several alternatives. Every _____ process produces a final choice. The output can be an action or an opinion of choice.

a. 529 plan
b. 4-4-5 Calendar
c. 7-Eleven
d. Decision making

14. A _____ is a decision support tool that uses a tree-like graph or model of decisions and their possible consequences, including chance event outcomes, resource costs, and utility. _____s are commonly used in operations research, specifically in decision analysis, to help identify a strategy most likely to reach a goal. Another use of _____s is as a descriptive means for calculating conditional probabilities.

a. 7-Eleven
b. 4-4-5 Calendar
c. 529 plan
d. Decision tree

15. _____ refers to the methods of practicing and using another person's business philosophy. The franchisor grants the independent operator the right to distribute its products, techniques, and trademarks for a percentage of gross monthly sales and a royalty fee. Various tangibles and intangibles such as national or international advertising, training, and other support services are commonly made available by the franchisor.

a. Franchising
b. 529 plan
c. 4-4-5 Calendar
d. 7-Eleven

16. A _____ is a form of partnership similar to a general partnership, except that in addition to one or more general partners (GPs), there are one or more limited partners (_____s). It is a partnership in which only one partner is required to be a general partner.

Chapter 3. The Business Plan

The GPs are, in all major respects, in the same legal position as partners in a conventional firm, i.e. they have management control, share the right to use partnership property, share the profits of the firm in predefined proportions, and have joint and several liability for the debts of the partnership.

- a. Limited liability company
- b. Limited partnership
- c. Leverage
- d. Fund of funds

17. _____ or net present worth (NPW) is defined as the total present value (PV) of a time series of cash flows. It is a standard method for using the time value of money to appraise long-term projects. Used for capital budgeting, and widely throughout economics, it measures the excess or shortfall of cash flows, in present value terms, once financing charges are met.
- a. Tax shield
- b. Present value of costs
- c. Negative gearing
- d. Net present value

18. A _____ is a type of business entity in which partners (owners) share with each other the profits or losses of the business undertaking in which all have invested. _____s are often favored over corporations for taxation purposes, as the _____ structure does not generally incur a tax on profits before it is distributed to the partners (i.e. there is no dividend tax levied.) However, depending on the _____ structure and the jurisdiction in which it operates, owners of a _____ may be exposed to greater personal liability than they would as shareholders of a corporation.
- a. Clayton Antitrust Act
- b. Fiduciary
- c. National Securities Markets Improvement Act of 1996
- d. Partnership

19. _____ is the value on a given date of a future payment or series of future payments, discounted to reflect the time value of money and other factors such as investment risk. _____ calculations are widely used in business and economics to provide a means to compare cash flows at different times on a meaningful 'like to like' basis.

The most commonly applied model of the time value of money is compound interest.

- a. Present value of benefits
- b. Present value
- c. Negative gearing
- d. Net present value

20. An _____ is a company whose main business is holding securities of other companies purely for investment purposes. The _____ invests money on behalf of its shareholders who in turn share in the profits and losses.
- a. A Random Walk Down Wall Street
- b. AAB
- c. Unit investment trust
- d. Investment Company

21. An _____ or angel is an affluent individual who provides capital for a business start-up, usually in exchange for convertible debt or ownership equity. A small but increasing number of _____s organize themselves into angel groups or angel networks to share research and pool their investment capital.

Angels typically invest their own funds, unlike venture capitalists, who manage the pooled money of others in a professionally-managed fund.

a. AAB
b. A Random Walk Down Wall Street
c. ABN Amro
d. Angel investor

22. _____ is an organization's process of defining its strategy and making decisions on allocating its resources to pursue this strategy, including its capital and people. Various business analysis techniques can be used in _____, including SWOT analysis (Strengths, Weaknesses, Opportunities, and Threats) and PEST analysis (Political, Economic, Social, and Technological analysis) or STEER analysis involving Socio-cultural, Technological, Economic, Ecological, and Regulatory factors and EPISTEL (Environment, Political, Informatic, Social, Technological, Economic and Legal)

_____ is the formal consideration of an organization's future course. All _____ deals with at least one of three key questions:

1. 'What do we do?'
2. 'For whom do we do it?'
3. 'How do we excel?'

In business _____, the third question is better phrased 'How can we beat or avoid competition?'. (Bradford and Duncan, page 1.)

a. 7-Eleven
b. 4-4-5 Calendar
c. 529 plan
d. Strategic planning

23. In the theory of capital structure, _____ is the phrase used to describe funds that firms obtain from outside of the firm. It is contrasted to internal financing which consists mainly of profits retained by the firm for investment. There are many kinds of _____.

a. Adjustment
b. Ownership equity
c. Asset-backed commercial paper
d. External financing

24. _____ or financing is to provide capital (funds), which means money for a project, a person, a business or any other private or public institutions.

Those funds can be allocated for either short term or long term purposes. The health fund is a new way of _____ private healthcare centers.

a. Product life cycle
b. Proxy fight
c. Synthetic CDO
d. Funding

25. _____ are business expenses that are not dependent on the level of production or sales. They tend to be time-related, such as salaries or rents being paid per month. This is in contrast to Variable costs, which are volume-related (and are paid per quantity.)

a. Marginal cost
b. Fixed costs
c. Sliding scale fees
d. Transaction cost

Chapter 3. The Business Plan

26. In economics and business decision-making, _____ are costs that cannot be recovered once they have been incurred. _____ are sometimes contrasted with variable costs, which are the costs that will change due to the proposed course of action, and prospective costs which are costs that will be incurred if an action is taken. In microeconomic theory, only variable costs are relevant to a decision.
    a. Hindsight bias
    b. Hyperbolic discounting
    c. 4-4-5 Calendar
    d. Sunk costs

27. The U.S. _____ is an independent agency of the United States government which holds primary responsibility for enforcing the federal securities laws and regulating the securities industry, the nation's stock and options exchanges, and other electronic securities markets. The SEC was created by section 4 of the SEC of 1934 (now codified as 15 U.S.C. Â§ 78d and commonly referred to as the 1934 Act.)
    a. 4-4-5 Calendar
    b. 7-Eleven
    c. 529 plan
    d. Securities and Exchange Commission

28. A _____ is an exchange of promises between two or more parties to do an act which is enforceable in a court of law. It is where an unqualified offer meets a qualified acceptance and the parties reach Consensus ad Idem. The parties must have the necessary capacity to _____ and the _____ must not be either trifling, indeterminate, impossible or illegal.
    a. 529 plan
    b. Contract
    c. 7-Eleven
    d. 4-4-5 Calendar

29. A '_____' is a 'Charge' that is paid to obtain the right to delay a payment. Essentially, the payer purchases the right to make a given payment in the future instead of in the Present. The '_____', or 'Charge' that must be paid to delay the payment, is simply the difference between what the payment amount would be if it were paid in the present and what the payment amount would be paid if it were paid in the future.
    a. Value at risk
    b. Risk aversion
    c. Risk modeling
    d. Discount

30. The _____ is an interest rate a central bank charges depository institutions that borrow reserves from it.

The term _____ has two meanings:

- the same as interest rate; the term 'discount' does not refer to the meaning of the word, but to the purpose of using the quantity, such as computations of present value, e.g. net present value / discounted cash flow

- the annual effective _____, which is the annual interest divided by the capital including that interest; this rate is lower than the interest rate; it corresponds to using the value after a year as the nominal value, and seeing the initial value as the nominal value minus a discount; it is used for Treasury Bills and similar financial instruments

The annual effective _____ is the annual interest divided by the capital including that interest, which is the interest rate divided by 100% plus the interest rate. It is the annual discount factor to be applied to the future cash flow, to find the discount, subtracted from a future value to find the value one year earlier.

For example, suppose there is a government bond that sells for $95 and pays $100 in a year's time.

a. Fisher equation
b. Black-Scholes
c. Stochastic volatility
d. Discount Rate

31. In business and accounting, _____s are everything of value that is owned by a person or company. The balance sheet of a firm records the monetary value of the _____s owned by the firm. The two major _____ classes are tangible _____s and intangible _____s.
   a. EBITDA
   b. Accounts payable
   c. Asset
   d. Income

32. In finance, _____ is the process of estimating the potential market value of a financial asset or liability. they can be done on assets (for example, investments in marketable securities such as stocks, options, business enterprises, or intangible assets such as patents and trademarks) or on liabilities (e.g., Bonds issued by a company.) _____s are required in many contexts including investment analysis, capital budgeting, merger and acquisition transactions, financial reporting, taxable events to determine the proper tax liability, and in litigation.
   a. Valuation
   b. Share
   c. Margin
   d. Procter ' Gamble

33. The term _____ has three unrelated technical definitions, and is also used in a variety of non-technical ways.

   - In financial economics, it refers to any asset used to make money, as opposed to assets used for personal enjoyment or consumption. This is an important distinction because two people can disagree sharply about the value of personal assets, one person might think a sports car is more valuable than a pickup truck, another person might have the opposite taste. But if an asset is held for the purpose of making money, taste has nothing to do with it, only differences of opinion about how much money the asset will produce. With the further assumption that people agree on the probability distribution of future cash flows, it is possible to have an objective _____ pricing model. Even without the assumption of agreement, it is possible to set rational limits on _____ value.
   - In governmental accounting, it is defined as any asset used in operations with an initial useful life extending beyond one reporting period. Generally, government managers have a 'stewardship' duty to maintain _____s under their control. See International Public Sector Accounting Standards for details.
   - In US tax accounting, it is defined as any property other than a list of exceptions. The main exceptions are anything held for sale, and any real estate or depreciable property used in business. Almost everything you own and use for personal purposes, pleasure or investment is a _____. If something is a _____ for tax purposes, gains or losses on sale or disposition are capital gains or capital losses. For individuals, however, capital losses on property held for personal use are generally not deductible. See the IRS publication Tax Facts about Capital Gains and Losses for details.

A well-known financial accounting textbook advises that the term be avoided except in tax accounting because it is used in so many different senses, not all of them well-defined. For example it is often used as a synonym for fixed assets or for investments in securities.

A common non-technical usage occurs when people ask that employees or the environment or something else be treated as a _____.

   a. Solvency
   b. Political risk
   c. Settlement date
   d. Capital Asset

34. In finance, the _____ is used to determine a theoretically appropriate required rate of return of an asset, if that asset is to be added to an already well-diversified portfolio, given that asset's non-diversifiable risk. The model takes into account the asset's sensitivity to non-diversifiable risk (also known as systemic risk or market risk), often represented by the quantity beta (β) in the financial industry, as well as the expected return of the market and the expected return of a theoretical risk-free asset.

The model was introduced by Jack Treynor (1961, 1962), William Sharpe (1964), John Lintner (1965a,b) and Jan Mossin (1966) independently, building on the earlier work of Harry Markowitz on diversification and modern portfolio theory.

   a. Hull-White model
   b. Cox-Ingersoll-Ross model
   c. Random walk hypothesis
   d. Capital Asset Pricing Model

35. In finance, _____ occurs when a debtor has not met its legal obligations according to the debt contract, e.g. it has not made a scheduled payment, or has violated a loan covenant (condition) of the debt contract. _____ may occur if the debtor is either unwilling or unable to pay their debt. This can occur with all debt obligations including bonds, mortgages, loans, and promissory notes.
   a. Credit crunch
   b. Vendor finance
   c. Debt validation
   d. Default

36. _____ is a term used for a number of concepts involving either the performance of an investigation of a business or person, or the performance of an act with a certain standard of care. It can be a legal obligation, but the term will more commonly apply to voluntary investigations. A common example of _____ in various industries is the process through which a potential acquirer evaluates a target company or its assets for acquisition.
   a. Bond indenture
   b. Quiet period
   c. Due diligence
   d. Down payment

Chapter 4. New Venture Strategy

1. A _____ is a corporation in the United States that, for Federal income tax purposes, is taxed under 26 U.S.C. Â§ 11 and Subchapter C (26 U.S.C. Â§ 11 and Subchapter C (26 U.S.C. Â§ 301 et seq.) of Chapter 1 of the Internal Revenue Code. Most major companies (and many smaller companies) are treated as _____ for Federal income tax purposes.

The income of a _____ is taxed, whereas the income of an S corporation (with a few exceptions) is not taxed under the Federal income tax laws. The income, or loss, is applied, Pro Rata, to each Shareholder and appears on their tax return as Schedule E income/(loss).

   a. 7-Eleven
   b. C corporation
   c. 4-4-5 Calendar
   d. 529 plan

2. An _____ is a contract written by a seller that conveys to the buyer the right -- but not the obligation -- to buy (in the case of a call _____) or to sell (in the case of a put _____) a particular asset, such as a piece of property such as, among others, a futures contract. In return for granting the _____, the seller collects a payment (the premium) from the buyer.

For example, buying a call _____ provides the right to buy a specified quantity of a security at a set strike price at some time on or before expiration, while buying a put _____ provides the right to sell.

   a. Annuity
   b. Amortization
   c. AT'T Mobility LLC
   d. Option

3. An _____ is a corporation that makes a valid election to be taxed under Subchapter S of Chapter 1 of the Internal Revenue Code.

In general, _____s do not pay any income taxes. Instead, the corporation's income or losses are divided among and passed through to its shareholders.

   a. 529 plan
   b. 4-4-5 Calendar
   c. 7-Eleven
   d. S corporation

4. _____ is a type of private equity capital typically provided to early-stage, high-potential, growth companies in the interest of generating a return through an eventual realization event such as an IPO or trade sale of the company. _____ investments are generally made as cash in exchange for shares in the invested company. It is typical for _____ investors to identify and back companies in high technology industries such as biotechnology and ICT.

   a. Tail risk
   b. Treasury Inflation-Protected Securities
   c. Venture Capital
   d. Probability distribution

5. The institution most often referenced by the word '_____' is a public or publicly traded _____, the shares of which are traded on a public stock exchange (e.g., the New York Stock Exchange or Nasdaq in the United States) where shares of stock of _____s are bought and sold by and to the general public. Most of the largest businesses in the world are publicly traded _____s. However, the majority of _____s are said to be closely held, privately held or close _____s, meaning that no ready market exists for the trading of shares.

   a. Federal Home Loan Mortgage Corporation
   b. Protect
   c. Depository Trust Company
   d. Corporation

Chapter 4. New Venture Strategy

6. In economics, business, and accounting, a _____ is the value of money that has been used up to produce something, and hence is not available for use anymore. In business, the _____ may be one of acquisition, in which case the amount of money expended to acquire it is counted as _____. In this case, money is the input that is gone in order to acquire the thing.
   a. Sliding scale fees
   b. Marginal cost
   c. Fixed costs
   d. Cost

7. The _____ is an expected return that the provider of capital plans to earn on their investment.

Capital (money) used for funding a business should earn returns for the capital providers who risk their capital. For an investment to be worthwhile, the expected return on capital must be greater than the _____.

   a. 4-4-5 Calendar
   b. Cost of capital
   c. Capital intensity
   d. Weighted average cost of capital

8. A _____ is a decision support tool that uses a tree-like graph or model of decisions and their possible consequences, including chance event outcomes, resource costs, and utility. _____s are commonly used in operations research, specifically in decision analysis, to help identify a strategy most likely to reach a goal. Another use of _____s is as a descriptive means for calculating conditional probabilities.
   a. 529 plan
   b. 4-4-5 Calendar
   c. 7-Eleven
   d. Decision tree

9. _____ is an organization's process of defining its strategy and making decisions on allocating its resources to pursue this strategy, including its capital and people. Various business analysis techniques can be used in _____, including SWOT analysis (Strengths, Weaknesses, Opportunities, and Threats) and PEST analysis (Political, Economic, Social, and Technological analysis) or STEER analysis involving Socio-cultural, Technological, Economic, Ecological, and Regulatory factors and EPISTEL (Environment, Political, Informatic, Social, Technological, Economic and Legal)

_____ is the formal consideration of an organization's future course. All _____ deals with at least one of three key questions:

   1. 'What do we do?'
   2. 'For whom do we do it?'
   3. 'How do we excel?'

In business _____, the third question is better phrased 'How can we beat or avoid competition?'. (Bradford and Duncan, page 1.)

   a. 7-Eleven
   b. Strategic planning
   c. 529 plan
   d. 4-4-5 Calendar

Chapter 4. New Venture Strategy

10. The term _____ refers to three closely related concepts:

- The _____ model is a mathematical model of the market for an equity, in which the equity's price is a stochastic process.
- The _____ PDE is a partial differential equation which (in the model) must be satisfied by the price of a derivative on the equity.
- The _____ formula is the result obtained by solving the _____ PDE for a European call option.

Fischer Black and Myron Scholes first articulated the _____ formula in their 1973 paper, 'The Pricing of Options and Corporate Liabilities.' The foundation for their research relied on work developed by scholars such as Jack L. Treynor, Paul Samuelson, A. James Boness, Sheen T. Kassouf, and Edward O. Thorp. The fundamental insight of _____ is that the option is implicitly priced if the stock is traded.

Robert C. Merton was the first to publish a paper expanding the mathematical understanding of the options pricing model and coined the term '_____' options pricing model.

a. Perpetuity
c. Modified Internal Rate of Return
b. Stochastic volatility
d. Black-Scholes

11. A _____ is a financial contract whose value is derived from the value of something else (known as the underlying.) The underlying on which a _____ is based can be an asset, weather conditions bonds or other forms of credit.
a. 7-Eleven
c. 529 plan
b. 4-4-5 Calendar
d. Derivative

12. _____ is a process of analyzing possible future events by considering alternative possible outcomes (scenarios.) The analysis is designed to allow improved decision-making by allowing consideration of outcomes and their implications.

For example, in economics and finance, a financial institution might attempt to forecast several possible scenarios for the economy (e.g. rapid growth, moderate growth, slow growth) and it might also attempt to forecast financial market returns (for bonds, stocks and cash) in each of those scenarios.

a. Scenario analysis
c. 4-4-5 Calendar
b. 529 plan
d. Detection Risk

13. The _____ of 1974 (Pub.L. 93-406, 88 Stat. 829, enacted September 2, 1974) is an American federal statute that establishes minimum standards for pension plans in private industry and provides for extensive rules on the federal income tax effects of transactions associated with employee benefit plans.
a. Articles of Partnership
c. Employee Retirement Income Security Act
b. Express warranty
d. Expedited Funds Availability Act

14. _____, refers to consumption opportunity gained by an entity within a specified time frame, which is generally expressed in monetary terms. However, for households and individuals, '_____ is the sum of all the wages, salaries, profits, interests payments, rents and other forms of earnings received... in a given period of time.' For firms, _____ generally refers to net-profit: what remains of revenue after expenses have been subtracted.

a. Annual report
b. Accrual
c. OIBDA
d. Income

15. A _____ is a fungible, negotiable instrument representing financial value. They are broadly categorized into debt securities (such as banknotes, bonds and debentures), and equity securities; e.g., common stocks. The company or other entity issuing the _____ is called the issuer.
   a. Tracking stock
   b. Book entry
   c. Security
   d. Securities lending

16. _____ or financing is to provide capital (funds), which means money for a project, a person, a business or any other private or public institutions.

Those funds can be allocated for either short term or long term purposes. The health fund is a new way of _____ private healthcare centers.

   a. Proxy fight
   b. Synthetic CDO
   c. Product life cycle
   d. Funding

17. A '_____' is a 'Charge' that is paid to obtain the right to delay a payment. Essentially, the payer purchases the right to make a given payment in the future instead of in the Present. The '_____', or 'Charge' that must be paid to delay the payment, is simply the difference between what the payment amount would be if it were paid in the present and what the payment amount would be paid if it were paid in the future.
   a. Value at risk
   b. Risk aversion
   c. Risk modeling
   d. Discount

18. The _____ is an interest rate a central bank charges depository institutions that borrow reserves from it.

The term _____ has two meanings:

- the same as interest rate; the term 'discount' does not refer to the meaning of the word, but to the purpose of using the quantity, such as computations of present value, e.g. net present value / discounted cash flow

- the annual effective _____, which is the annual interest divided by the capital including that interest; this rate is lower than the interest rate; it corresponds to using the value after a year as the nominal value, and seeing the initial value as the nominal value minus a discount; it is used for Treasury Bills and similar financial instruments

The annual effective _____ is the annual interest divided by the capital including that interest, which is the interest rate divided by 100% plus the interest rate. It is the annual discount factor to be applied to the future cash flow, to find the discount, subtracted from a future value to find the value one year earlier.

For example, suppose there is a government bond that sells for $95 and pays $100 in a year's time.

Chapter 4. New Venture Strategy

a. Stochastic volatility
b. Black-Scholes
c. Fisher equation
d. Discount Rate

19. A _____ is a pool of assets forming an independent legal entity that are bought with the contributions to a pension plan for the exclusive purpose of financing pension plan benefits.

_____s are important shareholders of listed and private companies. They are especially important to the stock market where large institutional investors like the Ontario Teachers' Pension Plan dominate.

a. Leveraged buyout
b. Leverage
c. Limited liability company
d. Pension fund

20. In economics, _____ is a measure of the relative satisfaction from or desirability of consumption of various goods and services. Given this measure, one may speak meaningfully of increasing or decreasing _____, and thereby explain economic behavior in terms of attempts to increase one's _____. For illustrative purposes, changes in _____ are sometimes expressed in units called utils.

a. A Random Walk Down Wall Street
b. AAB
c. Utility function
d. Utility

21. A _____ is a financial contract between two parties, the seller (writer) and the buyer of the option. The put allows its buyer the right but not the obligation to sell a commodity or financial instrument (the underlying instrument) to the writer (seller) of the option at a certain time for a certain price (the strike price.) The writer (seller) has the obligation to purchase the underlying asset at that strike price, if the buyer exercises the option.

a. Bear spread
b. Put option
c. Bear call spread
d. Debit spread

22. In corporate finance, _____ analysis applies put option and call option valuation techniques to capital budgeting decisions. A _____ itself, is the right--but not the obligation--to undertake some business decision; typically the option to make, or abandon, a capital investment. For example, the opportunity to invest in the expansion of a firm's factory, or alternatively to sell the factory, is a _____.

a. Cash flow
b. Real Option
c. Capital budgeting
d. Book building

23. _____ can be regarded as an outcome of mental processes (cognitive process) leading to the selection of a course of action among several alternatives. Every _____ process produces a final choice. The output can be an action or an opinion of choice.

a. Decision making
b. 7-Eleven
c. 4-4-5 Calendar
d. 529 plan

24. In the theory of capital structure, _____ is the phrase used to describe funds that firms obtain from outside of the firm. It is contrasted to internal financing which consists mainly of profits retained by the firm for investment. There are many kinds of _____.

a. Ownership equity
b. Adjustment
c. External financing
d. Asset-backed commercial paper

Chapter 4. New Venture Strategy

25. In business and accounting, _____s are everything of value that is owned by a person or company. The balance sheet of a firm records the monetary value of the _____s owned by the firm. The two major _____ classes are tangible _____s and intangible _____s.
    a. Asset
    b. Income
    c. Accounts payable
    d. EBITDA

26. In finance, _____ is the process of estimating the potential market value of a financial asset or liability. they can be done on assets (for example, investments in marketable securities such as stocks, options, business enterprises, or intangible assets such as patents and trademarks) or on liabilities (e.g., Bonds issued by a company.) _____s are required in many contexts including investment analysis, capital budgeting, merger and acquisition transactions, financial reporting, taxable events to determine the proper tax liability, and in litigation.
    a. Margin
    b. Procter ' Gamble
    c. Share
    d. Valuation

27. The term _____ has three unrelated technical definitions, and is also used in a variety of non-technical ways.

    - In financial economics, it refers to any asset used to make money, as opposed to assets used for personal enjoyment or consumption. This is an important distinction because two people can disagree sharply about the value of personal assets, one person might think a sports car is more valuable than a pickup truck, another person might have the opposite taste. But if an asset is held for the purpose of making money, taste has nothing to do with it, only differences of opinion about how much money the asset will produce. With the further assumption that people agree on the probability distribution of future cash flows, it is possible to have an objective _____ pricing model. Even without the assumption of agreement, it is possible to set rational limits on _____ value.
    - In governmental accounting, it is defined as any asset used in operations with an initial useful life extending beyond one reporting period. Generally, government managers have a 'stewardship' duty to maintain _____s under their control. See International Public Sector Accounting Standards for details.
    - In US tax accounting, it is defined as any property other than a list of exceptions. The main exceptions are anything held for sale, and any real estate or depreciable property used in business. Almost everything you own and use for personal purposes, pleasure or investment is a _____. If something is a _____ for tax purposes, gains or losses on sale or disposition are capital gains or capital losses. For individuals, however, capital losses on property held for personal use are generally not deductible. See the IRS publication Tax Facts about Capital Gains and Losses for details.

A well-known financial accounting textbook advises that the term be avoided except in tax accounting because it is used in so many different senses, not all of them well-defined. For example it is often used as a synonym for fixed assets or for investments in securities.

A common non-technical usage occurs when people ask that employees or the environment or something else be treated as a _____.

    a. Capital Asset
    b. Political risk
    c. Settlement date
    d. Solvency

Chapter 4. New Venture Strategy

28. In finance, the _____ is used to determine a theoretically appropriate required rate of return of an asset, if that asset is to be added to an already well-diversified portfolio, given that asset's non-diversifiable risk. The model takes into account the asset's sensitivity to non-diversifiable risk (also known as systemic risk or market risk), often represented by the quantity beta (β) in the financial industry, as well as the expected return of the market and the expected return of a theoretical risk-free asset.

The model was introduced by Jack Treynor (1961, 1962), William Sharpe (1964), John Lintner (1965a,b) and Jan Mossin (1966) independently, building on the earlier work of Harry Markowitz on diversification and modern portfolio theory.

a. Random walk hypothesis
b. Hull-White model
c. Cox-Ingersoll-Ross model
d. Capital Asset Pricing Model

29. In finance, _____ is the risk involved in using models to value financial securities. Rebonato considers alternative definitions including:

1) After observing a set of prices for the underlying and hedging instruments, different but identically calibrated models might produce different prices for the same exotic product. 2) Losses will be incurred because of an 'incorrect' hedging strategy suggested by a model.

a. Model risk
b. Duty of loyalty
c. Price-to-book ratio
d. Takeover

30. _____ are made by investors and investment managers.

Investors commonly perform investment analysis by making use of fundamental analysis, technical analysis and gut feel.

_____ are often supported by decision tools.

a. Asset allocation
b. Investment performance
c. Investing online
d. Investment decisions

31. A _____ is a payment made by a corporation to its shareholder members. When a corporation earns a profit or surplus, that money can be put to two uses: it can either be re-invested in the business (called retained earnings), or it can be paid to the shareholders as a _____. Many corporations retain a portion of their earnings and pay the remainder as a _____.

a. Dividend puzzle
b. Dividend
c. Dividend yield
d. Special dividend

Chapter 5. Developing Business Strategy Using Simulation

1. A _____ is a corporation in the United States that, for Federal income tax purposes, is taxed under 26 U.S.C. Â§ 11 and Subchapter C (26 U.S.C. Â§ 11 and Subchapter C (26 U.S.C. Â§ 301 et seq.) of Chapter 1 of the Internal Revenue Code. Most major companies (and many smaller companies) are treated as _____ for Federal income tax purposes.

The income of a _____ is taxed, whereas the income of an S corporation (with a few exceptions) is not taxed under the Federal income tax laws. The income, or loss, is applied, Pro Rata, to each Shareholder and appears on their tax return as Schedule E income/(loss).

   a. 4-4-5 Calendar
   b. 7-Eleven
   c. C corporation
   d. 529 plan

2. An _____ is a contract written by a seller that conveys to the buyer the right -- but not the obligation -- to buy (in the case of a call _____) or to sell (in the case of a put _____) a particular asset, such as a piece of property such as, among others, a futures contract. In return for granting the _____, the seller collects a payment (the premium) from the buyer.

For example, buying a call _____ provides the right to buy a specified quantity of a security at a set strike price at some time on or before expiration, while buying a put _____ provides the right to sell.

   a. Amortization
   b. Option
   c. AT'T Mobility LLC
   d. Annuity

3. An _____ is a corporation that makes a valid election to be taxed under Subchapter S of Chapter 1 of the Internal Revenue Code.

In general, _____s do not pay any income taxes. Instead, the corporation's income or losses are divided among and passed through to its shareholders.

   a. 4-4-5 Calendar
   b. S corporation
   c. 529 plan
   d. 7-Eleven

4. _____ is a type of private equity capital typically provided to early-stage, high-potential, growth companies in the interest of generating a return through an eventual realization event such as an IPO or trade sale of the company. _____ investments are generally made as cash in exchange for shares in the invested company. It is typical for _____ investors to identify and back companies in high technology industries such as biotechnology and ICT.

   a. Venture Capital
   b. Tail risk
   c. Probability distribution
   d. Treasury Inflation-Protected Securities

5. The institution most often referenced by the word '_____' is a public or publicly traded _____, the shares of which are traded on a public stock exchange (e.g., the New York Stock Exchange or Nasdaq in the United States) where shares of stock of _____s are bought and sold by and to the general public. Most of the largest businesses in the world are publicly traded _____s. However, the majority of _____s are said to be closely held, privately held or close _____s, meaning that no ready market exists for the trading of shares.

   a. Corporation
   b. Depository Trust Company
   c. Federal Home Loan Mortgage Corporation
   d. Protect

Chapter 5. Developing Business Strategy Using Simulation

6. In economics, business, and accounting, a _____ is the value of money that has been used up to produce something, and hence is not available for use anymore. In business, the _____ may be one of acquisition, in which case the amount of money expended to acquire it is counted as _____. In this case, money is the input that is gone in order to acquire the thing.
   a. Sliding scale fees
   b. Cost
   c. Marginal cost
   d. Fixed costs

7. The _____ is an expected return that the provider of capital plans to earn on their investment.

   Capital (money) used for funding a business should earn returns for the capital providers who risk their capital. For an investment to be worthwhile, the expected return on capital must be greater than the _____.

   a. Capital intensity
   b. Weighted average cost of capital
   c. 4-4-5 Calendar
   d. Cost of capital

8. The _____ of 1974 (Pub.L. 93-406, 88 Stat. 829, enacted September 2, 1974) is an American federal statute that establishes minimum standards for pension plans in private industry and provides for extensive rules on the federal income tax effects of transactions associated with employee benefit plans.
   a. Expedited Funds Availability Act
   b. Employee Retirement Income Security Act
   c. Articles of Partnership
   d. Express warranty

9. _____, refers to consumption opportunity gained by an entity within a specified time frame, which is generally expressed in monetary terms. However, for households and individuals, '_____ is the sum of all the wages, salaries, profits, interests payments, rents and other forms of earnings received... in a given period of time.' For firms, _____ generally refers to net-profit: what remains of revenue after expenses have been subtracted.
   a. Accrual
   b. Annual report
   c. Income
   d. OIBDA

10. A _____ is a fungible, negotiable instrument representing financial value. They are broadly categorized into debt securities (such as banknotes, bonds and debentures), and equity securities; e.g., common stocks. The company or other entity issuing the _____ is called the issuer.
    a. Securities lending
    b. Tracking stock
    c. Book entry
    d. Security

11. A '_____' is a 'Charge' that is paid to obtain the right to delay a payment. Essentially, the payer purchases the right to make a given payment in the future instead of in the Present. The '_____', or 'Charge' that must be paid to delay the payment, is simply the difference between what the payment amount would be if it were paid in the present and what the payment amount would be paid if it were paid in the future.
    a. Value at risk
    b. Risk modeling
    c. Discount
    d. Risk aversion

12. The _____ is an interest rate a central bank charges depository institutions that borrow reserves from it.

The term _____ has two meanings:

- the same as interest rate; the term 'discount' does not refer to the meaning of the word, but to the purpose of using the quantity, such as computations of present value, e.g. net present value / discounted cash flow

- the annual effective _____, which is the annual interest divided by the capital including that interest; this rate is lower than the interest rate; it corresponds to using the value after a year as the nominal value, and seeing the initial value as the nominal value minus a discount; it is used for Treasury Bills and similar financial instruments

The annual effective _____ is the annual interest divided by the capital including that interest, which is the interest rate divided by 100% plus the interest rate. It is the annual discount factor to be applied to the future cash flow, to find the discount, subtracted from a future value to find the value one year earlier.

For example, suppose there is a government bond that sells for $95 and pays $100 in a year's time.

a. Fisher equation
b. Black-Scholes
c. Stochastic volatility
d. Discount Rate

13. An _____ is a company whose main business is holding securities of other companies purely for investment purposes. The _____ invests money on behalf of its shareholders who in turn share in the profits and losses.
a. Unit investment trust
b. AAB
c. A Random Walk Down Wall Street
d. Investment company

14. The _____ is the market for securities, where companies and governments can raise longterm funds. The _____ includes the stock market and the bond market. Financial regulators, such as the U.S. Securities and Exchange Commission, oversee the _____s in their designated countries to ensure that investors are protected against fraud.
a. Delta neutral
b. Capital market
c. Forward market
d. Spot rate

15. In finance, a _____ is a security that entitles the holder to buy stock of the company that issued it at a specified price, which is usually higher than the stock price at time of issue.

_____s are frequently attached to bonds or preferred stock as a sweetener, allowing the issuer to pay lower interest rates or dividends. They can be used to enhance the yield of the bond, and make them more attractive to potential buyers.

a. Clearing
b. Clearing house
c. Credit
d. Warrant

16. The term _____ refers to three closely related concepts:

- The _____ model is a mathematical model of the market for an equity, in which the equity's price is a stochastic process.
- The _____ PDE is a partial differential equation which (in the model) must be satisfied by the price of a derivative on the equity.
- The _____ formula is the result obtained by solving the _____ PDE for a European call option.

Fischer Black and Myron Scholes first articulated the _____ formula in their 1973 paper, 'The Pricing of Options and Corporate Liabilities.' The foundation for their research relied on work developed by scholars such as Jack L. Treynor, Paul Samuelson, A. James Boness, Sheen T. Kassouf, and Edward O. Thorp. The fundamental insight of _____ is that the option is implicitly priced if the stock is traded.

Robert C. Merton was the first to publish a paper expanding the mathematical understanding of the options pricing model and coined the term '_____' options pricing model.

a. Perpetuity
c. Stochastic volatility

b. Black-Scholes
d. Modified Internal Rate of Return

Chapter 6. Methods of Financial Forecasting

1. A '_____' is a 'Charge' that is paid to obtain the right to delay a payment. Essentially, the payer purchases the right to make a given payment in the future instead of in the Present. The '_____', or 'Charge' that must be paid to delay the payment, is simply the difference between what the payment amount would be if it were paid in the present and what the payment amount would be paid if it were paid in the future.

   a. Value at risk
   b. Risk aversion
   c. Discount
   d. Risk modeling

2. The _____ is an interest rate a central bank charges depository institutions that borrow reserves from it.

The term _____ has two meanings:

- the same as interest rate; the term 'discount' does not refer to the meaning of the word, but to the purpose of using the quantity, such as computations of present value, e.g. net present value / discounted cash flow

- the annual effective _____, which is the annual interest divided by the capital including that interest; this rate is lower than the interest rate; it corresponds to using the value after a year as the nominal value, and seeing the initial value as the nominal value minus a discount; it is used for Treasury Bills and similar financial instruments

The annual effective _____ is the annual interest divided by the capital including that interest, which is the interest rate divided by 100% plus the interest rate. It is the annual discount factor to be applied to the future cash flow, to find the discount, subtracted from a future value to find the value one year earlier.

For example, suppose there is a government bond that sells for $95 and pays $100 in a year's time.

   a. Black-Scholes
   b. Discount Rate
   c. Fisher equation
   d. Stochastic volatility

3. The _____ of 1974 (Pub.L. 93-406, 88 Stat. 829, enacted September 2, 1974) is an American federal statute that establishes minimum standards for pension plans in private industry and provides for extensive rules on the federal income tax effects of transactions associated with employee benefit plans.

   a. Employee Retirement Income Security Act
   b. Express warranty
   c. Articles of Partnership
   d. Expedited Funds Availability Act

4. _____, refers to consumption opportunity gained by an entity within a specified time frame, which is generally expressed in monetary terms. However, for households and individuals, '_____ is the sum of all the wages, salaries, profits, interests payments, rents and other forms of earnings received... in a given period of time.' For firms, _____ generally refers to net-profit: what remains of revenue after expenses have been subtracted.

   a. Annual report
   b. Accrual
   c. Income
   d. OIBDA

5. An _____ is a contract written by a seller that conveys to the buyer the right -- but not the obligation -- to buy (in the case of a call _____) or to sell (in the case of a put _____) a particular asset, such as a piece of property such as, among others, a futures contract. In return for granting the _____, the seller collects a payment (the premium) from the buyer.

Chapter 6. Methods of Financial Forecasting 41

For example, buying a call _____ provides the right to buy a specified quantity of a security at a set strike price at some time on or before expiration, while buying a put _____ provides the right to sell.

a. Annuity
c. Amortization
b. AT'T Mobility LLC
d. Option

6. A _____ is a fungible, negotiable instrument representing financial value. They are broadly categorized into debt securities (such as banknotes, bonds and debentures), and equity securities; e.g., common stocks. The company or other entity issuing the _____ is called the issuer.

a. Book entry
c. Securities lending
b. Security
d. Tracking stock

7. _____ is a type of private equity capital typically provided to early-stage, high-potential, growth companies in the interest of generating a return through an eventual realization event such as an IPO or trade sale of the company. _____ investments are generally made as cash in exchange for shares in the invested company. It is typical for _____ investors to identify and back companies in high technology industries such as biotechnology and ICT.

a. Probability distribution
c. Treasury Inflation-Protected Securities
b. Tail risk
d. Venture Capital

8. _____ or financing is to provide capital (funds), which means money for a project, a person, a business or any other private or public institutions.

Those funds can be allocated for either short term or long term purposes. The health fund is a new way of _____ private healthcare centers.

a. Proxy fight
c. Product life cycle
b. Synthetic CDO
d. Funding

9. A _____ is a corporation in the United States that, for Federal income tax purposes, is taxed under 26 U.S.C. § 11 and Subchapter C (26 U.S.C. § 11 and Subchapter C (26 U.S.C. § 301 et seq.) of Chapter 1 of the Internal Revenue Code. Most major companies (and many smaller companies) are treated as _____ for Federal income tax purposes.

The income of a _____ is taxed, whereas the income of an S corporation (with a few exceptions) is not taxed under the Federal income tax laws. The income, or loss, is applied, Pro Rata, to each Shareholder and appears on their tax return as Schedule E income/(loss).

a. 4-4-5 Calendar
c. C corporation
b. 529 plan
d. 7-Eleven

10. An _____ is a corporation that makes a valid election to be taxed under Subchapter S of Chapter 1 of the Internal Revenue Code.

In general, _____s do not pay any income taxes. Instead, the corporation's income or losses are divided among and passed through to its shareholders.

a. 4-4-5 Calendar
c. 529 plan
b. S corporation
d. 7-Eleven

11. In financial accounting, a _____ or statement of financial position is a summary of a person's or organization's balances. Assets, liabilities and ownership equity are listed as of a specific date, such as the end of its financial year. A _____ is often described as a snapshot of a company's financial condition.
   a. Statement of retained earnings
   b. Financial statements
   c. Statement on Auditing Standards No. 70: Service Organizations
   d. Balance sheet

12. _____ is the balance of the amounts of cash being received and paid by a business during a defined period of time, sometimes tied to a specific project. Measurement of _____ can be used

   - to evaluate the state or performance of a business or project.
   - to determine problems with liquidity. Being profitable does not necessarily mean being liquid. A company can fail because of a shortage of cash, even while profitable.
   - to generate project rate of returns. The time of _____s into and out of projects are used as inputs to financial models such as internal rate of return, and net present value.
   - to examine income or growth of a business when it is believed that accrual accounting concepts do not represent economic realities. Alternately, _____ can be used to 'validate' the net income generated by accrual accounting.

   _____ as a generic term may be used differently depending on context, and certain _____ definitions may be adapted by analysts and users for their own uses. Common terms include operating _____ and free _____.

   _____s can be classified into:

   1. Operational _____s: Cash received or expended as a result of the company's core business activities.
   2. Investment _____s: Cash received or expended through capital expenditure, investments or acquisitions.
   3. Financing _____s: Cash received or expended as a result of financial activities, such as interests and dividends.

   All three together - the net _____ - are necessary to reconcile the beginning cash balance to the ending cash balance. Loan draw downs or equity injections, that is just shifting of capital but no expenditure as such, are not considered in the net _____.

   a. Cash flow
   b. Shareholder value
   c. Corporate finance
   d. Real option

13. The institution most often referenced by the word '_____' is a public or publicly traded _____, the shares of which are traded on a public stock exchange (e.g., the New York Stock Exchange or Nasdaq in the United States) where shares of stock of _____s are bought and sold by and to the general public. Most of the largest businesses in the world are publicly traded _____s. However, the majority of _____s are said to be closely held, privately held or close _____s, meaning that no ready market exists for the trading of shares.

Chapter 6. Methods of Financial Forecasting

a. Protect
b. Depository Trust Company
c. Federal Home Loan Mortgage Corporation
d. Corporation

14. In economics, business, and accounting, a _____ is the value of money that has been used up to produce something, and hence is not available for use anymore. In business, the _____ may be one of acquisition, in which case the amount of money expended to acquire it is counted as _____. In this case, money is the input that is gone in order to acquire the thing.
   a. Marginal cost
   b. Sliding scale fees
   c. Fixed costs
   d. Cost

15. The _____ is an expected return that the provider of capital plans to earn on their investment.

Capital (money) used for funding a business should earn returns for the capital providers who risk their capital. For an investment to be worthwhile, the expected return on capital must be greater than the _____.

   a. Capital intensity
   b. 4-4-5 Calendar
   c. Weighted average cost of capital
   d. Cost of capital

16. _____ are formal records of a business' financial activities.

_____ provide an overview of a business' financial condition in both short and long term. There are four basic _____:

   1. **Balance sheet**: also referred to as statement of financial position or condition, reports on a company's assets, liabilities, and net equity as of a given point in time.
   2. **Income statement**: also referred to as Profit and Loss statement (or a 'P'L'), reports on a company's income, expenses, and profits over a period of time.
   3. **Statement of retained earnings**: explains the changes in a company's retained earnings over the reporting period.
   4. **Statement of cash flows**: reports on a company's cash flow activities, particularly its operating, investing and financing activities.

   a. Notes to the Financial Statements
   b. Financial statements
   c. Statement of retained earnings
   d. Statement on Auditing Standards No. 70: Service Organizations

17. In accounting, _____ refers to the portion of net income which is retained by the corporation rather than distributed to its owners as dividends. Similarly, if the corporation makes a loss, then that loss is retained and called variously retained losses, accumulated losses or accumulated deficit. _____ and losses are cumulative from year to year with losses offsetting earnings.
   a. Retained earnings
   b. Generally Accepted Accounting Principles
   c. Historical cost
   d. Matching principle

44   *Chapter 6. Methods of Financial Forecasting*

18. In economic models, the _____ time frame assumes no fixed factors of production. Firms can enter or leave the marketplace, and the cost (and availability) of land, labor, raw materials, and capital goods can be assumed to vary. In contrast, in the short-run time frame, certain factors are assumed to be fixed, because there is not sufficient time for them to change.
    a. Long-run   b. 529 plan
    c. 4-4-5 Calendar   d. Short-run

19. In business and accounting, _____s are everything of value that is owned by a person or company. The balance sheet of a firm records the monetary value of the _____s owned by the firm. The two major _____ classes are tangible _____s and intangible _____s.
    a. EBITDA   b. Accounts payable
    c. Asset   d. Income

20. In finance, _____ is the process of estimating the potential market value of a financial asset or liability. they can be done on assets (for example, investments in marketable securities such as stocks, options, business enterprises, or intangible assets such as patents and trademarks) or on liabilities (e.g., Bonds issued by a company.) _____s are required in many contexts including investment analysis, capital budgeting, merger and acquisition transactions, financial reporting, taxable events to determine the proper tax liability, and in litigation.
    a. Procter ' Gamble   b. Valuation
    c. Margin   d. Share

21. The term _____ has three unrelated technical definitions, and is also used in a variety of non-technical ways.

- In financial economics, it refers to any asset used to make money, as opposed to assets used for personal enjoyment or consumption. This is an important distinction because two people can disagree sharply about the value of personal assets, one person might think a sports car is more valuable than a pickup truck, another person might have the opposite taste. But if an asset is held for the purpose of making money, taste has nothing to do with it, only differences of opinion about how much money the asset will produce. With the further assumption that people agree on the probability distribution of future cash flows, it is possible to have an objective _____ pricing model. Even without the assumption of agreement, it is possible to set rational limits on _____ value.
- In governmental accounting, it is defined as any asset used in operations with an initial useful life extending beyond one reporting period. Generally, government managers have a 'stewardship' duty to maintain _____s under their control. See International Public Sector Accounting Standards for details.
- In US tax accounting, it is defined as any property other than a list of exceptions. The main exceptions are anything held for sale, and any real estate or depreciable property used in business. Almost everything you own and use for personal purposes, pleasure or investment is a _____. If something is a _____ for tax purposes, gains or losses on sale or disposition are capital gains or capital losses. For individuals, however, capital losses on property held for personal use are generally not deductible. See the IRS publication Tax Facts about Capital Gains and Losses for details.

A well-known financial accounting textbook advises that the term be avoided except in tax accounting because it is used in so many different senses, not all of them well-defined. For example it is often used as a synonym for fixed assets or for investments in securities.

A common non-technical usage occurs when people ask that employees or the environment or something else be treated as a _____.

a. Settlement date   b. Solvency
c. Political risk   d. Capital Asset

22. In finance, the _____ is used to determine a theoretically appropriate required rate of return of an asset, if that asset is to be added to an already well-diversified portfolio, given that asset's non-diversifiable risk. The model takes into account the asset's sensitivity to non-diversifiable risk (also known as systemic risk or market risk), often represented by the quantity beta (β) in the financial industry, as well as the expected return of the market and the expected return of a theoretical risk-free asset.

The model was introduced by Jack Treynor (1961, 1962), William Sharpe (1964), John Lintner (1965a,b) and Jan Mossin (1966) independently, building on the earlier work of Harry Markowitz on diversification and modern portfolio theory.

a. Random walk hypothesis   b. Hull-White model
c. Capital Asset Pricing Model   d. Cox-Ingersoll-Ross model

23. An _____ is a company whose main business is holding securities of other companies purely for investment purposes. The _____ invests money on behalf of its shareholders who in turn share in the profits and losses.
a. Investment company   b. AAB
c. A Random Walk Down Wall Street   d. Unit investment trust

24. The _____ is the market for securities, where companies and governments can raise longterm funds. The _____ includes the stock market and the bond market. Financial regulators, such as the U.S. Securities and Exchange Commission, oversee the _____s in their designated countries to ensure that investors are protected against fraud.
a. Forward market   b. Spot rate
c. Capital market   d. Delta neutral

25. The _____ is the guaranteed payoff at which a person is 'indifferent' between accepting the guaranteed payoff and a higher but uncertain payoff. (It is the amount of the higher payout minus the risk premium).
a. 529 plan   b. Certainty equivalent
c. 7-Eleven   d. 4-4-5 Calendar

26. _____ is a list for goods and materials held available in stock by a business. It is also used for a list of the contents of a household and for a list for testamentary purposes of the possessions of someone who has died. In accounting _____ is considered an asset.
a. AAB   b. Inventory
c. ABN Amro   d. A Random Walk Down Wall Street

27. _____ right are usage-based payments made by one party to another (the 'licensor') for ongoing use of an asset, sometimes an intellectual property (IP) right..

_____ can be determined as a percentage of gross or net sales derived from use of the asset or a fixed price per unit sold. but there are also other modes and metrics of compensation.

a. Celler-Kefauver Act
b. Financial Institutions Reform Recovery and Enforcement Act
c. Due diligence
d. Royalties

28. _____ is a financial metric which represents operating liquidity available to a business. Along with fixed assets such as plant and equipment, _____ is considered a part of operating capital. It is calculated as current assets minus current liabilities.

a. 4-4-5 Calendar
b. Working capital management
c. 529 plan
d. Working capital

29. The _____ of a stock is a measure of the price paid for a share relative to the annual income or profit earned by the firm per share. It is a financial ratio used for valuation: a higher _____ means that investors are paying more for each unit of income, so the stock is more expensive compared to one with lower _____.

The _____ has units of years, which can be interpreted as 'number of years of earnings to pay back purchase price'.

a. Return of capital
b. Quick ratio
c. Sustainable growth rate
d. P/E ratio

30. _____ is an organization's process of defining its strategy and making decisions on allocating its resources to pursue this strategy, including its capital and people. Various business analysis techniques can be used in _____, including SWOT analysis (Strengths, Weaknesses, Opportunities, and Threats) and PEST analysis (Political, Economic, Social, and Technological analysis) or STEER analysis involving Socio-cultural, Technological, Economic, Ecological, and Regulatory factors and EPISTEL (Environment, Political, Informatic, Social, Technological, Economic and Legal)

_____ is the formal consideration of an organization's future course. All _____ deals with at least one of three key questions:

1. 'What do we do?'
2. 'For whom do we do it?'
3. 'How do we excel?'

In business _____, the third question is better phrased 'How can we beat or avoid competition?'. (Bradford and Duncan, page 1.)

a. 7-Eleven
b. 4-4-5 Calendar
c. 529 plan
d. Strategic planning

31. _____ refers to a business or organization attempting to acquire goods or services to accomplish the goals of the enterprise. Though there are several organizations that attempt to set standards in the _____ process, processes can vary greatly between organizations. Typically the word '_____' is not used interchangeably with the word 'procurement', since procurement typically includes Expediting, Supplier Quality, and Traffic and Logistics (T'L) in addition to _____.

a. 4-4-5 Calendar
b. 7-Eleven
c. 529 plan
d. Purchasing

Chapter 6. Methods of Financial Forecasting   47

32. _____, is when a company issues common stock or shares to the public for the first time. They are often issued by smaller, younger companies seeking capital to expand, but can also be done by large privately-owned companies looking to become publicly traded.

In an _____ the issuer may obtain the assistance of an underwriting firm, which helps it determine what type of security to issue (common or preferred), best offering price and time to bring it to market.

- a. Interest
- c. Insolvency
- b. Initial public offering
- d. Asian Financial Crisis

33. The term _____ is a term applied to practices that are perfunctory, or seek to satisfy the minimum requirements or to conform to a convention or doctrine. It has different meanings in different fields.

In accounting, _____ earnings are those earnings of companies in addition to actual earnings calculated under the Generally Accepted Accounting Principles (GAAP) in their quarterly and yearly financial reports.

- a. Long-term liabilities
- c. Pro forma
- b. Deferred financing costs
- d. Deferred income

34. An _____ is a financial statement for companies that indicates how Revenue is transformed into net income The purpose of the _____ is to show managers and investors whether the company made or lost money during the period being reported.

The important thing to remember about an _____ is that it represents a period of time.

- a. A Random Walk Down Wall Street
- c. Income statement
- b. AAB
- d. ABN Amro

35. The term _____ refers to three closely related concepts:

- The _____ model is a mathematical model of the market for an equity, in which the equity's price is a stochastic process.
- The _____ PDE is a partial differential equation which (in the model) must be satisfied by the price of a derivative on the equity.
- The _____ formula is the result obtained by solving the _____ PDE for a European call option.

Fischer Black and Myron Scholes first articulated the _____ formula in their 1973 paper, 'The Pricing of Options and Corporate Liabilities.' The foundation for their research relied on work developed by scholars such as Jack L. Treynor, Paul Samuelson, A. James Boness, Sheen T. Kassouf, and Edward O. Thorp. The fundamental insight of _____ is that the option is implicitly priced if the stock is traded.

Robert C. Merton was the first to publish a paper expanding the mathematical understanding of the options pricing model and coined the term '_____' options pricing model.

Chapter 6. Methods of Financial Forecasting

a. Stochastic volatility
c. Black-Scholes
b. Modified Internal Rate of Return
d. Perpetuity

36. _____ is the price at which an asset would trade in a competitive Walrasian auction setting. _____ is often used interchangeably with open _____, fair value or fair _____, although these terms have distinct definitions in different standards, and may differ in some circumstances.

International Valuation Standards defines _____ as 'the estimated amount for which a property should exchange on the date of valuation between a willing buyer and a willing seller in an arm'e;s-length transaction after proper marketing wherein the parties had each acted knowledgeably, prudently, and without compulsion.'

_____ is a concept distinct from market price, which is 'e;the price at which one can transact'e;, while _____ is 'e;the true underlying value'e; according to theoretical standards.

a. Debt restructuring
c. T-Model
b. Market value
d. Wrap account

37. In business, _____ is income that a company receives from its normal business activities, usually from the sale of goods and services to customers. Some companies also receive _____ from interest, dividends or royalties paid to them by other companies. _____ may refer to business income in general, or it may refer to the amount, in a monetary unit, received during a period of time, as in 'Last year, Company X had _____ of $32 million.'

In many countries, including the UK, _____ is referred to as turnover.

a. Bottom line
c. Furniture, Fixtures and Equipment
b. Matching principle
d. Revenue

38. The _____ or Venture Capital Method is a valuation method often used by venture capitalists and private equity professionals that combines elements of both a multiples-based valuation and a traditional discounted cash flow (DCF.) The method is particularly useful in valuing high-growth companies. Many practitioners feel that the method is better than a straight multiples method for valuing high-growth companies because high-growth companies do not have significant current financial results.

a. Sinking fund
c. Consumer basket
b. Risk-return spectrum
d. First Chicago method

39. _____, in bookkeeping, refers to assets, liabilities, income, and expenses recorded on individual pages of the so called book of final entry or ledger. Changes in _____ value are made by chronologically posting debit (DR) and credit (CR) entries to its page. Examples of _____s are cash, _____s receivable, mortgages, loans, land and buildings, common stock, sales, services provided, wages, and payroll overhead.

a. Option
c. Alpha
b. Accretion
d. Account

40. _____ is one of a series of accounting transactions dealing with the billing of customers who owe money to a person, company or organization for goods and services that have been provided to the customer. In most business entities this is typically done by generating an invoice and mailing or electronically delivering it to the customer, who in turn must pay it within an established timeframe called credit or payment terms.

Chapter 6. Methods of Financial Forecasting 49

An example of a common payment term is Net 30, meaning payment is due in the amount of the invoice 30 days from the date of invoice.

a. Impaired asset
b. Income
c. Accounting methods
d. Accounts receivable

41. The role of the _____ is to issue accounting standards in the United Kingdom. It is recognised for that purpose under the Companies Act 1985. It took over the task of setting accounting standards from the Accounting Standards Committee (ASC) in 1990.
a. AAB
b. ABN Amro
c. A Random Walk Down Wall Street
d. Accounting Standards Board

42. _____ is the field of accountancy concerned with the preparation of financial statements for decision makers, such as stockholders, suppliers, banks, employees, government agencies, owners, and other stakeholders. The fundamental need for _____ is to reduce principal-agent problem by measuring and monitoring agents' performance and reporting the results to interested users.

_____ is used to prepare accounting information for people outside the organization or not involved in the day to day running of the company.

a. 529 plan
b. 4-4-5 Calendar
c. Financial Accounting
d. 7-Eleven

43. The _____ is a private, not-for-profit organization whose primary purpose is to develop generally accepted accounting principles (GAAP) within the United States in the public's interest. The Securities and Exchange Commission (SEC) designated the _____ as the organization responsible for setting accounting standards for public companies in the U.S. It was created in 1973, replacing the Accounting Principles Board and the Committee on Accounting Procedure of the American Institute of Certified Public Accountants. The _____'s mission is 'to establish and improve standards of financial accounting and reporting for the guidance and education of the public, including issuers, auditors, and users of financial information.'

The _____ is not a governmental body.

a. Federal Deposit Insurance Corporation
b. World Congress of Accountants
c. KPMG
d. Financial Accounting Standards Board

44. The U.S. _____ is an independent agency of the United States government which holds primary responsibility for enforcing the federal securities laws and regulating the securities industry, the nation's stock and options exchanges, and other electronic securities markets. The SEC was created by section 4 of the SEC of 1934 (now codified as 15 U.S.C. § 78d and commonly referred to as the 1934 Act.)
a. Securities and Exchange Commission
b. 7-Eleven
c. 529 plan
d. 4-4-5 Calendar

Chapter 6. Methods of Financial Forecasting

45. An _____ or angel is an affluent individual who provides capital for a business start-up, usually in exchange for convertible debt or ownership equity. A small but increasing number of _____s organize themselves into angel groups or angel networks to share research and pool their investment capital.

Angels typically invest their own funds, unlike venture capitalists, who manage the pooled money of others in a professionally-managed fund.

a. ABN Amro
b. AAB
c. A Random Walk Down Wall Street
d. Angel investor

46. _____ is a legally declared inability or impairment of ability of an individual or organization to pay their creditors. Creditors may file a _____ petition against a debtor ('involuntary _____') in an effort to recoup a portion of what they are owed or initiate a restructuring. In the majority of cases, however, _____ is initiated by the debtor (a 'voluntary _____' that is filed by the bankrupt individual or organization.)

a. 4-4-5 Calendar
b. Debt settlement
c. Bankruptcy
d. 529 plan

47. _____ is the standard framework of guidelines for financial accounting used in the United States of America. It includes the standards, conventions, and rules accountants follow in recording and summarizing transactions, and in the preparation of financial statements. _____ are now issued by the Financial Accounting Standards Board (FASB).

a. Revenue
b. Net income
c. Depreciation
d. Generally accepted accounting principles

Chapter 7. Assessing Financial Needs

1. A _____ is a corporation in the United States that, for Federal income tax purposes, is taxed under 26 U.S.C. § 11 and Subchapter C (26 U.S.C. § 11 and Subchapter C (26 U.S.C. § 301 et seq.) of Chapter 1 of the Internal Revenue Code. Most major companies (and many smaller companies) are treated as _____ for Federal income tax purposes.

The income of a _____ is taxed, whereas the income of an S corporation (with a few exceptions) is not taxed under the Federal income tax laws. The income, or loss, is applied, Pro Rata, to each Shareholder and appears on their tax return as Schedule E income/(loss).

   a. C corporation
   b. 529 plan
   c. 7-Eleven
   d. 4-4-5 Calendar

2. The _____ of 1974 (Pub.L. 93-406, 88 Stat. 829, enacted September 2, 1974) is an American federal statute that establishes minimum standards for pension plans in private industry and provides for extensive rules on the federal income tax effects of transactions associated with employee benefit plans.

   a. Expedited Funds Availability Act
   b. Express warranty
   c. Articles of Partnership
   d. Employee Retirement Income Security Act

3. _____, refers to consumption opportunity gained by an entity within a specified time frame, which is generally expressed in monetary terms. However, for households and individuals, '_____ is the sum of all the wages, salaries, profits, interests payments, rents and other forms of earnings received... in a given period of time.' For firms, _____ generally refers to net-profit: what remains of revenue after expenses have been subtracted.

   a. Accrual
   b. Income
   c. Annual report
   d. OIBDA

4. An _____ is a corporation that makes a valid election to be taxed under Subchapter S of Chapter 1 of the Internal Revenue Code.

In general, _____s do not pay any income taxes. Instead, the corporation's income or losses are divided among and passed through to its shareholders.

   a. 4-4-5 Calendar
   b. 7-Eleven
   c. S corporation
   d. 529 plan

5. A _____ is a fungible, negotiable instrument representing financial value. They are broadly categorized into debt securities (such as banknotes, bonds and debentures), and equity securities; e.g., common stocks. The company or other entity issuing the _____ is called the issuer.

   a. Securities lending
   b. Book entry
   c. Security
   d. Tracking stock

6. _____ is a type of private equity capital typically provided to early-stage, high-potential, growth companies in the interest of generating a return through an eventual realization event such as an IPO or trade sale of the company. _____ investments are generally made as cash in exchange for shares in the invested company. It is typical for _____ investors to identify and back companies in high technology industries such as biotechnology and ICT.

   a. Treasury Inflation-Protected Securities
   b. Probability distribution
   c. Venture Capital
   d. Tail risk

Chapter 7. Assessing Financial Needs

7. _____ is the balance of the amounts of cash being received and paid by a business during a defined period of time, sometimes tied to a specific project. Measurement of _____ can be used

- to evaluate the state or performance of a business or project.
- to determine problems with liquidity. Being profitable does not necessarily mean being liquid. A company can fail because of a shortage of cash, even while profitable.
- to generate project rate of returns. The time of _____s into and out of projects are used as inputs to financial models such as internal rate of return, and net present value.
- to examine income or growth of a business when it is believed that accrual accounting concepts do not represent economic realities. Alternately, _____ can be used to 'validate' the net income generated by accrual accounting.

_____ as a generic term may be used differently depending on context, and certain _____ definitions may be adapted by analysts and users for their own uses. Common terms include operating _____ and free _____.

_____s can be classified into:

1. Operational _____s: Cash received or expended as a result of the company's core business activities.
2. Investment _____s: Cash received or expended through capital expenditure, investments or acquisitions.
3. Financing _____s: Cash received or expended as a result of financial activities, such as interests and dividends.

All three together - the net _____ - are necessary to reconcile the beginning cash balance to the ending cash balance. Loan draw downs or equity injections, that is just shifting of capital but no expenditure as such, are not considered in the net _____.

    a. Cash flow   b. Real option
    c. Corporate finance   d. Shareholder value

8. The institution most often referenced by the word '_____' is a public or publicly traded _____, the shares of which are traded on a public stock exchange (e.g., the New York Stock Exchange or Nasdaq in the United States) where shares of stock of _____s are bought and sold by and to the general public. Most of the largest businesses in the world are publicly traded _____s. However, the majority of _____s are said to be closely held, privately held or close _____s, meaning that no ready market exists for the trading of shares.

    a. Protect   b. Depository Trust Company
    c. Federal Home Loan Mortgage Corporation   d. Corporation

9. In economics, business, and accounting, a _____ is the value of money that has been used up to produce something, and hence is not available for use anymore. In business, the _____ may be one of acquisition, in which case the amount of money expended to acquire it is counted as _____. In this case, money is the input that is gone in order to acquire the thing.

    a. Sliding scale fees   b. Marginal cost
    c. Fixed costs   d. Cost

10. The _____ is an expected return that the provider of capital plans to earn on their investment.

Capital (money) used for funding a business should earn returns for the capital providers who risk their capital. For an investment to be worthwhile, the expected return on capital must be greater than the _____.

a. Capital intensity
b. 4-4-5 Calendar
c. Weighted average cost of capital
d. Cost of capital

11. _____ or financing is to provide capital (funds), which means money for a project, a person, a business or any other private or public institutions.

Those funds can be allocated for either short term or long term purposes. The health fund is a new way of _____ private healthcare centers.

a. Synthetic CDO
b. Proxy fight
c. Product life cycle
d. Funding

12. A _____ is a pool of assets forming an independent legal entity that are bought with the contributions to a pension plan for the exclusive purpose of financing pension plan benefits.

_____s are important shareholders of listed and private companies. They are especially important to the stock market where large institutional investors like the Ontario Teachers' Pension Plan dominate.

a. Leveraged buyout
b. Limited liability company
c. Leverage
d. Pension fund

13. An _____ is a company whose main business is holding securities of other companies purely for investment purposes. The _____ invests money on behalf of its shareholders who in turn share in the profits and losses.

a. Unit investment trust
b. AAB
c. A Random Walk Down Wall Street
d. Investment company

14. An _____ is a contract written by a seller that conveys to the buyer the right -- but not the obligation -- to buy (in the case of a call _____) or to sell (in the case of a put _____) a particular asset, such as a piece of property such as, among others, a futures contract. In return for granting the _____, the seller collects a payment (the premium) from the buyer.

For example, buying a call _____ provides the right to buy a specified quantity of a security at a set strike price at some time on or before expiration, while buying a put _____ provides the right to sell.

a. Annuity
b. Option
c. AT'T Mobility LLC
d. Amortization

15. The _____ is the market for securities, where companies and governments can raise longterm funds. The _____ includes the stock market and the bond market. Financial regulators, such as the U.S. Securities and Exchange Commission, oversee the _____s in their designated countries to ensure that investors are protected against fraud.

Chapter 7. Assessing Financial Needs

   a. Capital market   b. Forward market
   c. Spot rate   d. Delta neutral

16. In economics and contract theory, _____ deals with the study of decisions in transactions where one party has more or better information than the other. This creates an imbalance of power in transactions which can sometimes cause the transactions to go awry. Examples of this problem are adverse selection and moral hazard.
   a. ABN Amro   b. A Random Walk Down Wall Street
   c. AAB   d. Information asymmetry

17. In law, _____ refers to the process by which a company (or part of a company) is brought to an end, and the assets and property of the company redistributed. _____ can also be referred to as winding-up or dissolution, although dissolution technically refers to the last stage of _____. The process of _____ also arises when customs, an authority or agency in a country responsible for collecting and safeguarding customs duties, determines the final computation or ascertainment of the duties or drawback accruing on an entry.
   a. 529 plan   b. Debt settlement
   c. Liquidation   d. 4-4-5 Calendar

18. A _____ is a type of business entity in which partners (owners) share with each other the profits or losses of the business undertaking in which all have invested. _____s are often favored over corporations for taxation purposes, as the _____ structure does not generally incur a tax on profits before it is distributed to the partners (i.e. there is no dividend tax levied.) However, depending on the _____ structure and the jurisdiction in which it operates, owners of a _____ may be exposed to greater personal liability than they would as shareholders of a corporation.
   a. Fiduciary   b. National Securities Markets Improvement Act of 1996
   c. Clayton Antitrust Act   d. Partnership

19. In a company, _____ is the sum of all financial records of salaries, wages, bonuses and deductions.

A paycheck, is traditionally a paper document issued by an employer to pay an employee for services rendered. While most commonly used in the United States, recently the physical paycheck has been increasingly replaced by electronic direct deposit to bank accounts.

   a. Payroll   b. Tax expense
   c. 529 plan   d. 4-4-5 Calendar

20. A '_____' is a 'Charge' that is paid to obtain the right to delay a payment. Essentially, the payer purchases the right to make a given payment in the future instead of in the Present. The '_____', or 'Charge' that must be paid to delay the payment, is simply the difference between what the payment amount would be if it were paid in the present and what the payment amount would be paid if it were paid in the future.
   a. Risk aversion   b. Discount
   c. Risk modeling   d. Value at risk

21. The _____ is an interest rate a central bank charges depository institutions that borrow reserves from it.

Chapter 7. Assessing Financial Needs 55

The term _____ has two meanings:

- the same as interest rate; the term 'discount' does not refer to the meaning of the word, but to the purpose of using the quantity, such as computations of present value, e.g. net present value / discounted cash flow

- the annual effective _____, which is the annual interest divided by the capital including that interest; this rate is lower than the interest rate; it corresponds to using the value after a year as the nominal value, and seeing the initial value as the nominal value minus a discount; it is used for Treasury Bills and similar financial instruments

The annual effective _____ is the annual interest divided by the capital including that interest, which is the interest rate divided by 100% plus the interest rate. It is the annual discount factor to be applied to the future cash flow, to find the discount, subtracted from a future value to find the value one year earlier.

For example, suppose there is a government bond that sells for $95 and pays $100 in a year's time.

a. Stochastic volatility
c. Black-Scholes
b. Fisher equation
d. Discount Rate

22. _____ is that which is owed; usually referencing assets owed, but the term can cover other obligations. In the case of assets, _____ is a means of using future purchasing power in the present before a summation has been earned. Some companies and corporations use _____ as a part of their overall corporate finance strategy.
a. Credit cycle
c. Cross-collateralization
b. Partial Payment
d. Debt

23. _____ is an organization's process of defining its strategy and making decisions on allocating its resources to pursue this strategy, including its capital and people. Various business analysis techniques can be used in _____, including SWOT analysis (Strengths, Weaknesses, Opportunities, and Threats) and PEST analysis (Political, Economic, Social, and Technological analysis) or STEER analysis involving Socio-cultural, Technological, Economic, Ecological, and Regulatory factors and EPISTEL (Environment, Political, Informatic, Social, Technological, Economic and Legal)

_____ is the formal consideration of an organization's future course. All _____ deals with at least one of three key questions:

1. 'What do we do?'
2. 'For whom do we do it?'
3. 'How do we excel?'

In business _____, the third question is better phrased 'How can we beat or avoid competition?'. (Bradford and Duncan, page 1.)

a. 7-Eleven
c. 4-4-5 Calendar
b. 529 plan
d. Strategic planning

Chapter 7. Assessing Financial Needs

24. The term _____ refers to three closely related concepts:

   - The _____ model is a mathematical model of the market for an equity, in which the equity's price is a stochastic process.
   - The _____ PDE is a partial differential equation which (in the model) must be satisfied by the price of a derivative on the equity.
   - The _____ formula is the result obtained by solving the _____ PDE for a European call option.

Fischer Black and Myron Scholes first articulated the _____ formula in their 1973 paper, 'The Pricing of Options and Corporate Liabilities.' The foundation for their research relied on work developed by scholars such as Jack L. Treynor, Paul Samuelson, A. James Boness, Sheen T. Kassouf, and Edward O. Thorp. The fundamental insight of _____ is that the option is implicitly priced if the stock is traded.

Robert C. Merton was the first to publish a paper expanding the mathematical understanding of the options pricing model and coined the term '_____' options pricing model.

   a. Stochastic volatility
   b. Perpetuity
   c. Modified Internal Rate of Return
   d. Black-Scholes

25. In business and accounting, _____s are everything of value that is owned by a person or company. The balance sheet of a firm records the monetary value of the _____s owned by the firm. The two major _____ classes are tangible _____s and intangible _____s.

   a. EBITDA
   b. Income
   c. Accounts payable
   d. Asset

26. In finance, _____ is the process of estimating the potential market value of a financial asset or liability. they can be done on assets (for example, investments in marketable securities such as stocks, options, business enterprises, or intangible assets such as patents and trademarks) or on liabilities (e.g., Bonds issued by a company.) _____s are required in many contexts including investment analysis, capital budgeting, merger and acquisition transactions, financial reporting, taxable events to determine the proper tax liability, and in litigation.

   a. Share
   b. Valuation
   c. Procter ' Gamble
   d. Margin

Chapter 7. Assessing Financial Needs

27. The term _____ has three unrelated technical definitions, and is also used in a variety of non-technical ways.

- In financial economics, it refers to any asset used to make money, as opposed to assets used for personal enjoyment or consumption. This is an important distinction because two people can disagree sharply about the value of personal assets, one person might think a sports car is more valuable than a pickup truck, another person might have the opposite taste. But if an asset is held for the purpose of making money, taste has nothing to do with it, only differences of opinion about how much money the asset will produce. With the further assumption that people agree on the probability distribution of future cash flows, it is possible to have an objective _____ pricing model. Even without the assumption of agreement, it is possible to set rational limits on _____ value.
- In governmental accounting, it is defined as any asset used in operations with an initial useful life extending beyond one reporting period. Generally, government managers have a 'stewardship' duty to maintain _____s under their control. See International Public Sector Accounting Standards for details.
- In US tax accounting, it is defined as any property other than a list of exceptions. The main exceptions are anything held for sale, and any real estate or depreciable property used in business. Almost everything you own and use for personal purposes, pleasure or investment is a _____. If something is a _____ for tax purposes, gains or losses on sale or disposition are capital gains or capital losses. For individuals, however, capital losses on property held for personal use are generally not deductible. See the IRS publication Tax Facts about Capital Gains and Losses for details.

A well-known financial accounting textbook advises that the term be avoided except in tax accounting because it is used in so many different senses, not all of them well-defined. For example it is often used as a synonym for fixed assets or for investments in securities.

A common non-technical usage occurs when people ask that employees or the environment or something else be treated as a _____.

a. Settlement date
c. Political risk

b. Solvency
d. Capital Asset

28. In finance, the _____ is used to determine a theoretically appropriate required rate of return of an asset, if that asset is to be added to an already well-diversified portfolio, given that asset's non-diversifiable risk. The model takes into account the asset's sensitivity to non-diversifiable risk (also known as systemic risk or market risk), often represented by the quantity beta (β) in the financial industry, as well as the expected return of the market and the expected return of a theoretical risk-free asset.

The model was introduced by Jack Treynor (1961, 1962), William Sharpe (1964), John Lintner (1965a,b) and Jan Mossin (1966) independently, building on the earlier work of Harry Markowitz on diversification and modern portfolio theory.

a. Hull-White model
c. Cox-Ingersoll-Ross model

b. Random walk hypothesis
d. Capital Asset Pricing Model

29. The _____ is the guaranteed payoff at which a person is 'indifferent' between accepting the guaranteed payoff and a higher but uncertain payoff. (It is the amount of the higher payout minus the risk premium).

Chapter 7. Assessing Financial Needs

a. 529 plan
b. 4-4-5 Calendar
c. 7-Eleven
d. Certainty equivalent

30. _____ right are usage-based payments made by one party to another (the 'licensor') for ongoing use of an asset, sometimes an intellectual property (IP) right..

_____ can be determined as a percentage of gross or net sales derived from use of the asset or a fixed price per unit sold. but there are also other modes and metrics of compensation.

a. Celler-Kefauver Act
b. Royalties
c. Financial Institutions Reform Recovery and Enforcement Act
d. Due diligence

31. _____ is a process of analyzing possible future events by considering alternative possible outcomes (scenarios.) The analysis is designed to allow improved decision-making by allowing consideration of outcomes and their implications.

For example, in economics and finance, a financial institution might attempt to forecast several possible scenarios for the economy (e.g. rapid growth, moderate growth, slow growth) and it might also attempt to forecast financial market returns (for bonds, stocks and cash) in each of those scenarios.

a. Detection Risk
b. 4-4-5 Calendar
c. 529 plan
d. Scenario analysis

32. _____ is the study of how the variation (uncertainty) in the output of a mathematical model can be apportioned, qualitatively or quantitatively, to different sources of variation in the input of a model .

In more general terms uncertainty and sensitivity analyses investigate the robustness of a study when the study includes some form of mathematical modelling. While uncertainty analysis studies the overall uncertainty in the conclusions of the study, _____ tries to identify what source of uncertainty weights more on the study's conclusions.

a. Proxy fight
b. Golden parachute
c. Sensitivity analysis
d. Synthetic CDO

Chapter 8. The Framework of New Venture Valuation

1. In business and accounting, _____s are everything of value that is owned by a person or company. The balance sheet of a firm records the monetary value of the _____s owned by the firm. The two major _____ classes are tangible _____s and intangible _____s.
   a. Accounts payable
   b. Income
   c. EBITDA
   d. Asset

2. In finance, _____ is the process of estimating the potential market value of a financial asset or liability. they can be done on assets (for example, investments in marketable securities such as stocks, options, business enterprises, or intangible assets such as patents and trademarks) or on liabilities (e.g., Bonds issued by a company.) _____s are required in many contexts including investment analysis, capital budgeting, merger and acquisition transactions, financial reporting, taxable events to determine the proper tax liability, and in litigation.
   a. Share
   b. Procter ' Gamble
   c. Margin
   d. Valuation

3. The term _____ has three unrelated technical definitions, and is also used in a variety of non-technical ways.

   - In financial economics, it refers to any asset used to make money, as opposed to assets used for personal enjoyment or consumption. This is an important distinction because two people can disagree sharply about the value of personal assets, one person might think a sports car is more valuable than a pickup truck, another person might have the opposite taste. But if an asset is held for the purpose of making money, taste has nothing to do with it, only differences of opinion about how much money the asset will produce. With the further assumption that people agree on the probability distribution of future cash flows, it is possible to have an objective _____ pricing model. Even without the assumption of agreement, it is possible to set rational limits on _____ value.
   - In governmental accounting, it is defined as any asset used in operations with an initial useful life extending beyond one reporting period. Generally, government managers have a 'stewardship' duty to maintain _____s under their control. See International Public Sector Accounting Standards for details.
   - In US tax accounting, it is defined as any property other than a list of exceptions. The main exceptions are anything held for sale, and any real estate or depreciable property used in business. Almost everything you own and use for personal purposes, pleasure or investment is a _____. If something is a _____ for tax purposes, gains or losses on sale or disposition are capital gains or capital losses. For individuals, however, capital losses on property held for personal use are generally not deductible. See the IRS publication Tax Facts about Capital Gains and Losses for details.

A well-known financial accounting textbook advises that the term be avoided except in tax accounting because it is used in so many different senses, not all of them well-defined. For example it is often used as a synonym for fixed assets or for investments in securities.

A common non-technical usage occurs when people ask that employees or the environment or something else be treated as a _____.

   a. Settlement date
   b. Political risk
   c. Solvency
   d. Capital Asset

Chapter 8. The Framework of New Venture Valuation

4. In finance, the _____ is used to determine a theoretically appropriate required rate of return of an asset, if that asset is to be added to an already well-diversified portfolio, given that asset's non-diversifiable risk. The model takes into account the asset's sensitivity to non-diversifiable risk (also known as systemic risk or market risk), often represented by the quantity beta (β) in the financial industry, as well as the expected return of the market and the expected return of a theoretical risk-free asset.

The model was introduced by Jack Treynor (1961, 1962), William Sharpe (1964), John Lintner (1965a,b) and Jan Mossin (1966) independently, building on the earlier work of Harry Markowitz on diversification and modern portfolio theory.

- a. Hull-White model
- b. Cox-Ingersoll-Ross model
- c. Capital Asset Pricing Model
- d. Random walk hypothesis

5. An _____ is a contract written by a seller that conveys to the buyer the right -- but not the obligation -- to buy (in the case of a call _____) or to sell (in the case of a put _____) a particular asset, such as a piece of property such as, among others, a futures contract. In return for granting the _____, the seller collects a payment (the premium) from the buyer.

For example, buying a call _____ provides the right to buy a specified quantity of a security at a set strike price at some time on or before expiration, while buying a put _____ provides the right to sell.

- a. Amortization
- b. Annuity
- c. AT'T Mobility LLC
- d. Option

6. _____ is a type of private equity capital typically provided to early-stage, high-potential, growth companies in the interest of generating a return through an eventual realization event such as an IPO or trade sale of the company. _____ investments are generally made as cash in exchange for shares in the invested company. It is typical for _____ investors to identify and back companies in high technology industries such as biotechnology and ICT.

- a. Tail risk
- b. Treasury Inflation-Protected Securities
- c. Probability distribution
- d. Venture Capital

7. In economics, business, and accounting, a _____ is the value of money that has been used up to produce something, and hence is not available for use anymore. In business, the _____ may be one of acquisition, in which case the amount of money expended to acquire it is counted as _____. In this case, money is the input that is gone in order to acquire the thing.

- a. Marginal cost
- b. Fixed costs
- c. Cost
- d. Sliding scale fees

8. The _____ is an expected return that the provider of capital plans to earn on their investment.

Capital (money) used for funding a business should earn returns for the capital providers who risk their capital. For an investment to be worthwhile, the expected return on capital must be greater than the _____.

- a. Weighted average cost of capital
- b. 4-4-5 Calendar
- c. Capital intensity
- d. Cost of capital

Chapter 8. The Framework of New Venture Valuation

9. A _____ is a corporation in the United States that, for Federal income tax purposes, is taxed under 26 U.S.C. § 11 and Subchapter C (26 U.S.C. § 11 and Subchapter C (26 U.S.C. § 301 et seq.) of Chapter 1 of the Internal Revenue Code. Most major companies (and many smaller companies) are treated as _____ for Federal income tax purposes.

The income of a _____ is taxed, whereas the income of an S corporation (with a few exceptions) is not taxed under the Federal income tax laws. The income, or loss, is applied, Pro Rata, to each Shareholder and appears on their tax return as Schedule E income/(loss).

    a. C corporation   b. 529 plan
    c. 4-4-5 Calendar   d. 7-Eleven

10. A '_____' is a 'Charge' that is paid to obtain the right to delay a payment. Essentially, the payer purchases the right to make a given payment in the future instead of in the Present. The '_____', or 'Charge' that must be paid to delay the payment, is simply the difference between what the payment amount would be if it were paid in the present and what the payment amount would be paid if it were paid in the future.

    a. Value at risk   b. Risk modeling
    c. Discount   d. Risk aversion

11. The _____ is an interest rate a central bank charges depository institutions that borrow reserves from it.

The term _____ has two meanings:

- the same as interest rate; the term 'discount' does not refer to the meaning of the word, but to the purpose of using the quantity, such as computations of present value, e.g. net present value / discounted cash flow

- the annual effective _____, which is the annual interest divided by the capital including that interest; this rate is lower than the interest rate; it corresponds to using the value after a year as the nominal value, and seeing the initial value as the nominal value minus a discount; it is used for Treasury Bills and similar financial instruments

The annual effective _____ is the annual interest divided by the capital including that interest, which is the interest rate divided by 100% plus the interest rate. It is the annual discount factor to be applied to the future cash flow, to find the discount, subtracted from a future value to find the value one year earlier.

For example, suppose there is a government bond that sells for $95 and pays $100 in a year's time.

    a. Black-Scholes   b. Stochastic volatility
    c. Discount Rate   d. Fisher equation

12. An _____ is a corporation that makes a valid election to be taxed under Subchapter S of Chapter 1 of the Internal Revenue Code.

In general, _____s do not pay any income taxes. Instead, the corporation's income or losses are divided among and passed through to its shareholders.

Chapter 8. The Framework of New Venture Valuation

a. 7-Eleven
b. 529 plan
c. 4-4-5 Calendar
d. S corporation

13. The institution most often referenced by the word '_____' is a public or publicly traded _____, the shares of which are traded on a public stock exchange (e.g., the New York Stock Exchange or Nasdaq in the United States) where shares of stock of _____s are bought and sold by and to the general public. Most of the largest businesses in the world are publicly traded _____s. However, the majority of _____s are said to be closely held, privately held or close _____s, meaning that no ready market exists for the trading of shares.
  a. Protect
  b. Federal Home Loan Mortgage Corporation
  c. Depository Trust Company
  d. Corporation

14. _____ is a mathematical science pertaining to the collection, analysis, interpretation or explanation, and presentation of data. It also provides tools for prediction and forecasting based on data. It is applicable to a wide variety of academic disciplines, from the natural and social sciences to the humanities, government and business.
  a. Sample size
  b. Covariance
  c. Mean
  d. Statistics

15. In finance, the value of an option consists of two components, its intrinsic value and its _____. Time value is simply the difference between option value and intrinsic value. _____ is also known as theta, extrinsic value, or instrumental value.
  a. Global Squeeze
  b. Conservatism
  c. Debt buyer
  d. Time value

16. The _____ of 1974 (Pub.L. 93-406, 88 Stat. 829, enacted September 2, 1974) is an American federal statute that establishes minimum standards for pension plans in private industry and provides for extensive rules on the federal income tax effects of transactions associated with employee benefit plans.
  a. Articles of Partnership
  b. Employee Retirement Income Security Act
  c. Express warranty
  d. Expedited Funds Availability Act

17. _____, refers to consumption opportunity gained by an entity within a specified time frame, which is generally expressed in monetary terms. However, for households and individuals, '_____ is the sum of all the wages, salaries, profits, interests payments, rents and other forms of earnings received... in a given period of time.' For firms, _____ generally refers to net-profit: what remains of revenue after expenses have been subtracted.
  a. Income
  b. OIBDA
  c. Annual report
  d. Accrual

18. A _____ is a fungible, negotiable instrument representing financial value. They are broadly categorized into debt securities (such as banknotes, bonds and debentures), and equity securities; e.g., common stocks. The company or other entity issuing the _____ is called the issuer.
  a. Securities lending
  b. Tracking stock
  c. Book entry
  d. Security

19. In finance, _____, also known as return on investment is the ratio of money gained or lost on an investment relative to the amount of money invested. The amount of money gained or lost may be referred to as interest, profit/loss, gain/loss, or net income/loss. The money invested may be referred to as the asset, capital, principal, or the cost basis of the investment.

Chapter 8. The Framework of New Venture Valuation

a. Doctrine of the Proper Law
c. Rate of return

b. Compbsiition of Creditors
d. Stock or scrip dividends

20. _____, is when a company issues common stock or shares to the public for the first time. They are often issued by smaller, younger companies seeking capital to expand, but can also be done by large privately-owned companies looking to become publicly traded.

In an _____ the issuer may obtain the assistance of an underwriting firm, which helps it determine what type of security to issue (common or preferred), best offering price and time to bring it to market.

a. Asian Financial Crisis
c. Insolvency

b. Interest
d. Initial public offering

21. _____ proposes how rational investors will use diversification to optimize their portfolios, and how a risky asset should be priced. The basic concepts of the theory are Markowitz diversification, the efficient frontier, capital asset pricing model, the alpha and beta coefficients, the Capital Market Line and the Securities Market Line.

_____ models an asset's return as a random variable, and models a portfolio as a weighted combination of assets so that the return of a portfolio is the weighted combination of the assets' returns.

a. Consumer basket
c. Market value

b. Modern portfolio theory
d. Payback period

22. The _____ is the guaranteed payoff at which a person is 'indifferent' between accepting the guaranteed payoff and a higher but uncertain payoff. (It is the amount of the higher payout minus the risk premium).

a. 529 plan
c. 7-Eleven

b. 4-4-5 Calendar
d. Certainty equivalent

23. _____ is the balance of the amounts of cash being received and paid by a business during a defined period of time, sometimes tied to a specific project. Measurement of _____ can be used

- to evaluate the state or performance of a business or project.
- to determine problems with liquidity. Being profitable does not necessarily mean being liquid. A company can fail because of a shortage of cash, even while profitable.
- to generate project rate of returns. The time of _____s into and out of projects are used as inputs to financial models such as internal rate of return, and net present value.
- to examine income or growth of a business when it is believed that accrual accounting concepts do not represent economic realities. Alternately, _____ can be used to 'validate' the net income generated by accrual accounting.

_____ as a generic term may be used differently depending on context, and certain _____ definitions may be adapted by analysts and users for their own uses. Common terms include operating _____ and free _____.

64 Chapter 8. The Framework of New Venture Valuation

_____s can be classified into:

1. Operational _____s: Cash received or expended as a result of the company's core business activities.
2. Investment _____s: Cash received or expended through capital expenditure, investments or acquisitions.
3. Financing _____s: Cash received or expended as a result of financial activities, such as interests and dividends.

All three together - the net _____ - are necessary to reconcile the beginning cash balance to the ending cash balance. Loan draw downs or equity injections, that is just shifting of capital but no expenditure as such, are not considered in the net _____.

a. Shareholder value
c. Cash flow
b. Real option
d. Corporate finance

24. The _____ of a stock is a measure of the price paid for a share relative to the annual income or profit earned by the firm per share. It is a financial ratio used for valuation: a higher _____ means that investors are paying more for each unit of income, so the stock is more expensive compared to one with lower _____.

The _____ has units of years, which can be interpreted as 'number of years of earnings to pay back purchase price'.

a. Sustainable growth rate
c. Return of capital
b. P/E ratio
d. Quick ratio

25. _____ in finance is a risk management technique, related to hedging, that mixes a wide variety of investments within a portfolio. Because the fluctuations of a single security have less impact on a diverse portfolio, _____ minimizes the risk from any one investment.

A simple example of _____ is the following: On a particular island the entire economy consists of two companies: one that sells umbrellas and another that sells sunscreen.

a. 4-4-5 Calendar
c. 7-Eleven
b. 529 plan
d. Diversification

26. A _____ is a financial contract between two parties, the seller (writer) and the buyer of the option. The put allows its buyer the right but not the obligation to sell a commodity or financial instrument (the underlying instrument) to the writer (seller) of the option at a certain time for a certain price (the strike price.) The writer (seller) has the obligation to purchase the underlying asset at that strike price, if the buyer exercises the option.

a. Debit spread
c. Put option
b. Bear call spread
d. Bear spread

Chapter 8. The Framework of New Venture Valuation

27. In economics and finance, _____ is the practice of taking advantage of a price differential between two or more markets: striking a combination of matching deals that capitalize upon the imbalance, the profit being the difference between the market prices. When used by academics, an _____ is a transaction that involves no negative cash flow at any probabilistic or temporal state and a positive cash flow in at least one state; in simple terms, a risk-free profit.

a. Initial margin
b. Arbitrage
c. Efficient-market hypothesis
d. Issuer

Chapter 9. Valuation in Practice: The Investor's Perspective

1. In business and accounting, _____s are everything of value that is owned by a person or company. The balance sheet of a firm records the monetary value of the _____s owned by the firm. The two major _____ classes are tangible _____s and intangible _____s.
   a. EBITDA
   b. Income
   c. Accounts payable
   d. Asset

2. In finance, _____ is the process of estimating the potential market value of a financial asset or liability. they can be done on assets (for example, investments in marketable securities such as stocks, options, business enterprises, or intangible assets such as patents and trademarks) or on liabilities (e.g., Bonds issued by a company.) _____s are required in many contexts including investment analysis, capital budgeting, merger and acquisition transactions, financial reporting, taxable events to determine the proper tax liability, and in litigation.
   a. Margin
   b. Procter ' Gamble
   c. Share
   d. Valuation

3. The term _____ has three unrelated technical definitions, and is also used in a variety of non-technical ways.

   - In financial economics, it refers to any asset used to make money, as opposed to assets used for personal enjoyment or consumption. This is an important distinction because two people can disagree sharply about the value of personal assets, one person might think a sports car is more valuable than a pickup truck, another person might have the opposite taste. But if an asset is held for the purpose of making money, taste has nothing to do with it, only differences of opinion about how much money the asset will produce. With the further assumption that people agree on the probability distribution of future cash flows, it is possible to have an objective _____ pricing model. Even without the assumption of agreement, it is possible to set rational limits on _____ value.
   - In governmental accounting, it is defined as any asset used in operations with an initial useful life extending beyond one reporting period. Generally, government managers have a 'stewardship' duty to maintain _____s under their control. See International Public Sector Accounting Standards for details.
   - In US tax accounting, it is defined as any property other than a list of exceptions. The main exceptions are anything held for sale, and any real estate or depreciable property used in business. Almost everything you own and use for personal purposes, pleasure or investment is a _____. If something is a _____ for tax purposes, gains or losses on sale or disposition are capital gains or capital losses. For individuals, however, capital losses on property held for personal use are generally not deductible. See the IRS publication Tax Facts about Capital Gains and Losses for details.

   A well-known financial accounting textbook advises that the term be avoided except in tax accounting because it is used in so many different senses, not all of them well-defined. For example it is often used as a synonym for fixed assets or for investments in securities.

   A common non-technical usage occurs when people ask that employees or the environment or something else be treated as a _____.

   a. Settlement date
   b. Political risk
   c. Capital Asset
   d. Solvency

Chapter 9. Valuation in Practice: The Investor's Perspective

4. In finance, the _____ is used to determine a theoretically appropriate required rate of return of an asset, if that asset is to be added to an already well-diversified portfolio, given that asset's non-diversifiable risk. The model takes into account the asset's sensitivity to non-diversifiable risk (also known as systemic risk or market risk), often represented by the quantity beta (β) in the financial industry, as well as the expected return of the market and the expected return of a theoretical risk-free asset.

The model was introduced by Jack Treynor (1961, 1962), William Sharpe (1964), John Lintner (1965a,b) and Jan Mossin (1966) independently, building on the earlier work of Harry Markowitz on diversification and modern portfolio theory.

- a. Hull-White model
- b. Cox-Ingersoll-Ross model
- c. Random walk hypothesis
- d. Capital Asset Pricing Model

5. A '_____' is a 'Charge' that is paid to obtain the right to delay a payment. Essentially, the payer purchases the right to make a given payment in the future instead of in the Present. The '_____', or 'Charge' that must be paid to delay the payment, is simply the difference between what the payment amount would be if it were paid in the present and what the payment amount would be paid if it were paid in the future.

- a. Value at risk
- b. Risk modeling
- c. Discount
- d. Risk aversion

6. The _____ is an interest rate a central bank charges depository institutions that borrow reserves from it.

The term _____ has two meanings:

- the same as interest rate; the term 'discount' does not refer to the meaning of the word, but to the purpose of using the quantity, such as computations of present value, e.g. net present value / discounted cash flow

- the annual effective _____, which is the annual interest divided by the capital including that interest; this rate is lower than the interest rate; it corresponds to using the value after a year as the nominal value, and seeing the initial value as the nominal value minus a discount; it is used for Treasury Bills and similar financial instruments

The annual effective _____ is the annual interest divided by the capital including that interest, which is the interest rate divided by 100% plus the interest rate. It is the annual discount factor to be applied to the future cash flow, to find the discount, subtracted from a future value to find the value one year earlier.

For example, suppose there is a government bond that sells for $95 and pays $100 in a year's time.

- a. Stochastic volatility
- b. Black-Scholes
- c. Fisher equation
- d. Discount Rate

7. The _____ of 1974 (Pub.L. 93-406, 88 Stat. 829, enacted September 2, 1974) is an American federal statute that establishes minimum standards for pension plans in private industry and provides for extensive rules on the federal income tax effects of transactions associated with employee benefit plans.

Chapter 9. Valuation in Practice: The Investor's Perspective

a. Expedited Funds Availability Act
b. Employee Retirement Income Security Act
c. Articles of Partnership
d. Express warranty

8. The _____ or Venture Capital Method is a valuation method often used by venture capitalists and private equity professionals that combines elements of both a multiples-based valuation and a traditional discounted cash flow (DCF.) The method is particularly useful in valuing high-growth companies. Many practitioners feel that the method is better than a straight multiples method for valuing high-growth companies because high-growth companies do not have significant current financial results.

a. Risk-return spectrum
b. Consumer basket
c. First Chicago method
d. Sinking fund

9. _____, refers to consumption opportunity gained by an entity within a specified time frame, which is generally expressed in monetary terms. However, for households and individuals, '_____ is the sum of all the wages, salaries, profits, interests payments, rents and other forms of earnings received... in a given period of time.' For firms, _____ generally refers to net-profit: what remains of revenue after expenses have been subtracted.

a. Annual report
b. Income
c. OIBDA
d. Accrual

10. An _____ is a contract written by a seller that conveys to the buyer the right -- but not the obligation -- to buy (in the case of a call _____) or to sell (in the case of a put _____) a particular asset, such as a piece of property such as, among others, a futures contract. In return for granting the _____, the seller collects a payment (the premium) from the buyer.

For example, buying a call _____ provides the right to buy a specified quantity of a security at a set strike price at some time on or before expiration, while buying a put _____ provides the right to sell.

a. AT'T Mobility LLC
b. Annuity
c. Option
d. Amortization

11. A _____ is a fungible, negotiable instrument representing financial value. They are broadly categorized into debt securities (such as banknotes, bonds and debentures), and equity securities; e.g., common stocks. The company or other entity issuing the _____ is called the issuer.

a. Book entry
b. Tracking stock
c. Security
d. Securities lending

12. _____ is a type of private equity capital typically provided to early-stage, high-potential, growth companies in the interest of generating a return through an eventual realization event such as an IPO or trade sale of the company. _____ investments are generally made as cash in exchange for shares in the invested company. It is typical for _____ investors to identify and back companies in high technology industries such as biotechnology and ICT.

a. Tail risk
b. Venture Capital
c. Treasury Inflation-Protected Securities
d. Probability distribution

13. In economics, business, and accounting, a _____ is the value of money that has been used up to produce something, and hence is not available for use anymore. In business, the _____ may be one of acquisition, in which case the amount of money expended to acquire it is counted as _____. In this case, money is the input that is gone in order to acquire the thing.

Chapter 9. Valuation in Practice: The Investor's Perspective

a. Marginal cost
c. Fixed costs
b. Sliding scale fees
d. Cost

14. The _____ is an expected return that the provider of capital plans to earn on their investment.

Capital (money) used for funding a business should earn returns for the capital providers who risk their capital. For an investment to be worthwhile, the expected return on capital must be greater than the _____.

a. Weighted average cost of capital
c. Capital intensity
b. 4-4-5 Calendar
d. Cost of capital

15. _____ is the balance of the amounts of cash being received and paid by a business during a defined period of time, sometimes tied to a specific project. Measurement of _____ can be used

- to evaluate the state or performance of a business or project.
- to determine problems with liquidity. Being profitable does not necessarily mean being liquid. A company can fail because of a shortage of cash, even while profitable.
- to generate project rate of returns. The time of _____s into and out of projects are used as inputs to financial models such as internal rate of return, and net present value.
- to examine income or growth of a business when it is believed that accrual accounting concepts do not represent economic realities. Alternately, _____ can be used to 'validate' the net income generated by accrual accounting.

_____ as a generic term may be used differently depending on context, and certain _____ definitions may be adapted by analysts and users for their own uses. Common terms include operating _____ and free _____.

_____s can be classified into:

1. Operational _____s: Cash received or expended as a result of the company's core business activities.
2. Investment _____s: Cash received or expended through capital expenditure, investments or acquisitions.
3. Financing _____s: Cash received or expended as a result of financial activities, such as interests and dividends.

All three together - the net _____ - are necessary to reconcile the beginning cash balance to the ending cash balance. Loan draw downs or equity injections, that is just shifting of capital but no expenditure as such, are not considered in the net _____.

a. Cash flow
c. Shareholder value
b. Real option
d. Corporate finance

Chapter 9. Valuation in Practice: The Investor`s Perspective

16. In finance, the _____ (continuing value or horizon value) of a security is the present value at a future point in time of all future cash flows when we expect stable growth rate forever. It is most often used in multi-stage discounted cash flow analysis, and allows for the limitation of cash flow projections to a several-year period. Forecasting results beyond such a period is impractical and exposes such projections to a variety of risks limiting their validity, primarily the great uncertainty involved in predicting industry and macroeconomic conditions beyond a few years.
   a. Negative gearing
   b. Discounted cash flow
   c. Refinancing risk
   d. Terminal value

17. _____, is when a company issues common stock or shares to the public for the first time. They are often issued by smaller, younger companies seeking capital to expand, but can also be done by large privately-owned companies looking to become publicly traded.

   In an _____ the issuer may obtain the assistance of an underwriting firm, which helps it determine what type of security to issue (common or preferred), best offering price and time to bring it to market.

   a. Asian Financial Crisis
   b. Insolvency
   c. Interest
   d. Initial public offering

18. The _____ of a stock is a measure of the price paid for a share relative to the annual income or profit earned by the firm per share. It is a financial ratio used for valuation: a higher _____ means that investors are paying more for each unit of income, so the stock is more expensive compared to one with lower _____.

   The _____ has units of years, which can be interpreted as 'number of years of earnings to pay back purchase price'.

   a. Return of capital
   b. Sustainable growth rate
   c. Quick ratio
   d. P/E ratio

19. _____ is typically a higher ranking stock than voting shares, and its terms are negotiated between the corporation and the investor.

   _____ usually carry no voting rights, but may carry superior priority over common stock in the payment of dividends and upon liquidation. _____ may carry a dividend that is paid out prior to any dividends to common stock holders.

   a. Preferred stock
   b. Trade-off theory
   c. Follow-on offering
   d. Second lien loan

20. _____ is a mathematical science pertaining to the collection, analysis, interpretation or explanation, and presentation of data. It also provides tools for prediction and forecasting based on data. It is applicable to a wide variety of academic disciplines, from the natural and social sciences to the humanities, government and business.
   a. Covariance
   b. Sample size
   c. Mean
   d. Statistics

Chapter 9. Valuation in Practice: The Investor's Perspective

21. The term _____ refers to three closely related concepts:

- The _____ model is a mathematical model of the market for an equity, in which the equity's price is a stochastic process.
- The _____ PDE is a partial differential equation which (in the model) must be satisfied by the price of a derivative on the equity.
- The _____ formula is the result obtained by solving the _____ PDE for a European call option.

Fischer Black and Myron Scholes first articulated the _____ formula in their 1973 paper, 'The Pricing of Options and Corporate Liabilities.' The foundation for their research relied on work developed by scholars such as Jack L. Treynor, Paul Samuelson, A. James Boness, Sheen T. Kassouf, and Edward O. Thorp. The fundamental insight of _____ is that the option is implicitly priced if the stock is traded.

Robert C. Merton was the first to publish a paper expanding the mathematical understanding of the options pricing model and coined the term '_____' options pricing model.

a. Stochastic volatility
c. Perpetuity
b. Modified Internal Rate of Return
d. Black-Scholes

22. A _____ is a corporation in the United States that, for Federal income tax purposes, is taxed under 26 U.S.C. § 11 and Subchapter C (26 U.S.C. § 11 and Subchapter C (26 U.S.C. § 301 et seq.) of Chapter 1 of the Internal Revenue Code. Most major companies (and many smaller companies) are treated as _____ for Federal income tax purposes.

The income of a _____ is taxed, whereas the income of an S corporation (with a few exceptions) is not taxed under the Federal income tax laws. The income, or loss, is applied, Pro Rata, to each Shareholder and appears on their tax return as Schedule E income/(loss).

a. 529 plan
c. 7-Eleven
b. 4-4-5 Calendar
d. C corporation

23. In finance, a _____ is a debt security, in which the authorized issuer owes the holders a debt and, depending on the terms of the _____, is obliged to pay interest (the coupon) and/or to repay the principal at a later date, termed maturity.

Thus a _____ is a loan: the issuer is the borrower, the _____ holder is the lender, and the coupon is the interest. _____s provide the borrower with external funds to finance long-term investments, or, in the case of government _____s, to finance current expenditure.

a. Puttable bond
c. Catastrophe bonds
b. Bond
d. Convertible bond

24. A _____ is a financial contract between two parties, the buyer and the seller of this type of option. Often it is simply labeled a 'call'. The buyer of the option has the right, but not the obligation to buy an agreed quantity of a particular commodity or financial instrument (the underlying instrument) from the seller of the option at a certain time (the expiration date) for a certain price (the strike price.)

a. Bull spread
b. Call option
c. Bear call spread
d. Bear spread

25. The institution most often referenced by the word '_____' is a public or publicly traded _____, the shares of which are traded on a public stock exchange (e.g., the New York Stock Exchange or Nasdaq in the United States) where shares of stock of _____s are bought and sold by and to the general public. Most of the largest businesses in the world are publicly traded _____s. However, the majority of _____s are said to be closely held, privately held or close _____s, meaning that no ready market exists for the trading of shares.

a. Depository Trust Company
b. Protect
c. Federal Home Loan Mortgage Corporation
d. Corporation

26. _____ or financing is to provide capital (funds), which means money for a project, a person, a business or any other private or public institutions.

Those funds can be allocated for either short term or long term purposes. The health fund is a new way of _____ private healthcare centers.

a. Product life cycle
b. Proxy fight
c. Synthetic CDO
d. Funding

27. _____ is a fee paid on borrowed assets. It is the price paid for the use of borrowed money, or, money earned by deposited funds. Assets that are sometimes lent with _____ include money, shares, consumer goods through hire purchase, major assets such as aircraft, and even entire factories in finance lease arrangements.

a. A Random Walk Down Wall Street
b. Insolvency
c. Interest
d. AAB

28. An _____ is the price a borrower pays for the use of money they do not own, and the return a lender receives for deferring the use of funds, by lending it to the borrower. _____s are normally expressed as a percentage rate over the period of one year.

_____s targets are also a vital tool of monetary policy and are used to control variables like investment, inflation, and unemployment.

a. ABN Amro
b. AAB
c. A Random Walk Down Wall Street
d. Interest rate

29. In finance, _____ is that risk which is common to an entire market and not to any individual entity or component thereof. It should be distinguished from systemic risk which is the risk that the entire financial system will collapse as a result of some catastrophic event.

Risks can be reduced in four main ways: Avoidance, Reduction, Retention and Transfer.

a. Capital surplus
b. Primary market
c. Conglomerate merger
d. Systematic risk

Chapter 9. Valuation in Practice: The Investor's Perspective

30. The _____ is a United States government system for classifying industries by a four-digit code. Established in 1937, it is being supplanted by the six-digit North American Industry Classification System, which was released in 1997; however certain government departments and agencies, such as the U.S. Securities and Exchange Commission (SEC), still use the _____ codes.

The following table is from the SEC's site, which allows searching for companies by _____ code in its database of filings.

a. 7-Eleven
b. 529 plan
c. Standard Industrial Classification
d. 4-4-5 Calendar

31. In finance, _____, also known as return on investment is the ratio of money gained or lost on an investment relative to the amount of money invested. The amount of money gained or lost may be referred to as interest, profit/loss, gain/loss, or net income/loss. The money invested may be referred to as the asset, capital, principal, or the cost basis of the investment.
a. Stock or scrip dividends
b. Composiition of Creditors
c. Doctrine of the Proper Law
d. Rate of return

32. The _____ is the guaranteed payoff at which a person is 'indifferent' between accepting the guaranteed payoff and a higher but uncertain payoff. (It is the amount of the higher payout minus the risk premium).
a. 529 plan
b. Certainty equivalent
c. 7-Eleven
d. 4-4-5 Calendar

33. _____ right are usage-based payments made by one party to another (the 'licensor') for ongoing use of an asset, sometimes an intellectual property (IP) right..

_____ can be determined as a percentage of gross or net sales derived from use of the asset or a fixed price per unit sold. but there are also other modes and metrics of compensation.

a. Financial Institutions Reform Recovery and Enforcement Act
b. Celler-Kefauver Act
c. Due diligence
d. Royalties

34. An _____ is a company whose main business is holding securities of other companies purely for investment purposes. The _____ invests money on behalf of its shareholders who in turn share in the profits and losses.
a. Unit investment trust
b. AAB
c. Investment Company
d. A Random Walk Down Wall Street

35. An _____ is a corporation that makes a valid election to be taxed under Subchapter S of Chapter 1 of the Internal Revenue Code.

In general, _____s do not pay any income taxes. Instead, the corporation's income or losses are divided among and passed through to its shareholders.

a. 4-4-5 Calendar
c. 7-Eleven
b. 529 plan
d. S corporation

36. _____ is a measure of the ability of a debtor to pay their debts as and when they fall due. It is usually expressed as a ratio or a percentage of current liabilities.

For a corporation with a published balance sheet there are various ratios used to calculate a measure of liquidity.

a. Operating leverage
c. Accounting liquidity
b. Operating profit margin
d. Invested capital

37. A _____ is a payment made by a corporation to its shareholder members. When a corporation earns a profit or surplus, that money can be put to two uses: it can either be re-invested in the business (called retained earnings), or it can be paid to the shareholders as a _____. Many corporations retain a portion of their earnings and pay the remainder as a _____.

a. Dividend puzzle
c. Special dividend
b. Dividend
d. Dividend yield

Chapter 10. Valuation: The Entrepreneur's Perspective

1. A _____ is a corporation in the United States that, for Federal income tax purposes, is taxed under 26 U.S.C. § 11 and Subchapter C (26 U.S.C. § 11 and Subchapter C (26 U.S.C. § 301 et seq.) of Chapter 1 of the Internal Revenue Code. Most major companies (and many smaller companies) are treated as _____ for Federal income tax purposes.

The income of a _____ is taxed, whereas the income of an S corporation (with a few exceptions) is not taxed under the Federal income tax laws. The income, or loss, is applied, Pro Rata, to each Shareholder and appears on their tax return as Schedule E income/(loss).

   a. 4-4-5 Calendar
   b. 7-Eleven
   c. 529 plan
   d. C corporation

2. A '_____' is a 'Charge' that is paid to obtain the right to delay a payment. Essentially, the payer purchases the right to make a given payment in the future instead of in the Present. The '_____', or 'Charge' that must be paid to delay the payment, is simply the difference between what the payment amount would be if it were paid in the present and what the payment amount would be paid if it were paid in the future.

   a. Risk aversion
   b. Discount
   c. Risk modeling
   d. Value at risk

3. The _____ is an interest rate a central bank charges depository institutions that borrow reserves from it.

The term _____ has two meanings:

   - the same as interest rate; the term 'discount' does not refer to the meaning of the word, but to the purpose of using the quantity, such as computations of present value, e.g. net present value / discounted cash flow

   - the annual effective _____, which is the annual interest divided by the capital including that interest; this rate is lower than the interest rate; it corresponds to using the value after a year as the nominal value, and seeing the initial value as the nominal value minus a discount; it is used for Treasury Bills and similar financial instruments

The annual effective _____ is the annual interest divided by the capital including that interest, which is the interest rate divided by 100% plus the interest rate. It is the annual discount factor to be applied to the future cash flow, to find the discount, subtracted from a future value to find the value one year earlier.

For example, suppose there is a government bond that sells for $95 and pays $100 in a year's time.

   a. Stochastic volatility
   b. Fisher equation
   c. Discount Rate
   d. Black-Scholes

4. The _____ of 1974 (Pub.L. 93-406, 88 Stat. 829, enacted September 2, 1974) is an American federal statute that establishes minimum standards for pension plans in private industry and provides for extensive rules on the federal income tax effects of transactions associated with employee benefit plans.

   a. Articles of Partnership
   b. Employee Retirement Income Security Act
   c. Expedited Funds Availability Act
   d. Express warranty

Chapter 10. Valuation: The Entrepreneur`s Perspective

5. _____, refers to consumption opportunity gained by an entity within a specified time frame, which is generally expressed in monetary terms. However, for households and individuals, '_____ is the sum of all the wages, salaries, profits, interests payments, rents and other forms of earnings received... in a given period of time.' For firms, _____ generally refers to net-profit: what remains of revenue after expenses have been subtracted.
   a. Annual report
   b. Income
   c. OIBDA
   d. Accrual

6. An _____ is a contract written by a seller that conveys to the buyer the right -- but not the obligation -- to buy (in the case of a call _____) or to sell (in the case of a put _____) a particular asset, such as a piece of property such as, among others, a futures contract. In return for granting the _____, the seller collects a payment (the premium) from the buyer.

For example, buying a call _____ provides the right to buy a specified quantity of a security at a set strike price at some time on or before expiration, while buying a put _____ provides the right to sell.

   a. Option
   b. Annuity
   c. AT'T Mobility LLC
   d. Amortization

7. An _____ is a corporation that makes a valid election to be taxed under Subchapter S of Chapter 1 of the Internal Revenue Code.

In general, _____s do not pay any income taxes. Instead, the corporation's income or losses are divided among and passed through to its shareholders.

   a. 4-4-5 Calendar
   b. S corporation
   c. 7-Eleven
   d. 529 plan

8. A _____ is a fungible, negotiable instrument representing financial value. They are broadly categorized into debt securities (such as banknotes, bonds and debentures), and equity securities; e.g., common stocks. The company or other entity issuing the _____ is called the issuer.
   a. Book entry
   b. Tracking stock
   c. Security
   d. Securities lending

9. _____ is a type of private equity capital typically provided to early-stage, high-potential, growth companies in the interest of generating a return through an eventual realization event such as an IPO or trade sale of the company. _____ investments are generally made as cash in exchange for shares in the invested company. It is typical for _____ investors to identify and back companies in high technology industries such as biotechnology and ICT.
   a. Probability distribution
   b. Treasury Inflation-Protected Securities
   c. Venture Capital
   d. Tail risk

10. The institution most often referenced by the word '_____' is a public or publicly traded _____, the shares of which are traded on a public stock exchange (e.g., the New York Stock Exchange or Nasdaq in the United States) where shares of stock of _____s are bought and sold by and to the general public. Most of the largest businesses in the world are publicly traded _____s. However, the majority of _____s are said to be closely held, privately held or close _____s, meaning that no ready market exists for the trading of shares.

Chapter 10. Valuation: The Entrepreneur's Perspective

a. Protect
c. Depository Trust Company
b. Federal Home Loan Mortgage Corporation
d. Corporation

11. In economics, business, and accounting, a _____ is the value of money that has been used up to produce something, and hence is not available for use anymore. In business, the _____ may be one of acquisition, in which case the amount of money expended to acquire it is counted as _____. In this case, money is the input that is gone in order to acquire the thing.
   a. Fixed costs
   c. Sliding scale fees
   b. Marginal cost
   d. Cost

12. The _____ is an expected return that the provider of capital plans to earn on their investment.

Capital (money) used for funding a business should earn returns for the capital providers who risk their capital. For an investment to be worthwhile, the expected return on capital must be greater than the _____.

   a. Capital intensity
   c. 4-4-5 Calendar
   b. Weighted average cost of capital
   d. Cost of capital

13. In finance, _____ is the process of estimating the potential market value of a financial asset or liability. they can be done on assets (for example, investments in marketable securities such as stocks, options, business enterprises, or intangible assets such as patents and trademarks) or on liabilities (e.g., Bonds issued by a company.) _____s are required in many contexts including investment analysis, capital budgeting, merger and acquisition transactions, financial reporting, taxable events to determine the proper tax liability, and in litigation.
   a. Valuation
   c. Margin
   b. Share
   d. Procter ' Gamble

14. _____ in finance is a risk management technique, related to hedging, that mixes a wide variety of investments within a portfolio. Because the fluctuations of a single security have less impact on a diverse portfolio, _____ minimizes the risk from any one investment.

A simple example of _____ is the following: On a particular island the entire economy consists of two companies: one that sells umbrellas and another that sells sunscreen.

   a. Diversification
   c. 4-4-5 Calendar
   b. 7-Eleven
   d. 529 plan

15. _____ or economic opportunity loss is the value of the next best alternative foregone as the result of making a decision. _____ analysis is an important part of a company's decision-making processes but is not treated as an actual cost in any financial statement. The next best thing that a person can engage in is referred to as the _____ of doing the best thing and ignoring the next best thing to be done.
   a. ABN Amro
   c. AAB
   b. A Random Walk Down Wall Street
   d. Opportunity cost

16. An _____ is a company whose main business is holding securities of other companies purely for investment purposes. The _____ invests money on behalf of its shareholders who in turn share in the profits and losses.

a. A Random Walk Down Wall Street   b. AAB
c. Unit investment trust   d. Investment Company

17. A _____ is an exchange of promises between two or more parties to do an act which is enforceable in a court of law. It is where an unqualified offer meets a qualified acceptance and the parties reach Consensus ad Idem. The parties must have the necessary capacity to _____ and the _____ must not be either trifling, indeterminate, impossible or illegal.
   a. 7-Eleven   b. 4-4-5 Calendar
   c. Contract   d. 529 plan

18. In business and accounting, _____s are everything of value that is owned by a person or company. The balance sheet of a firm records the monetary value of the _____s owned by the firm. The two major _____ classes are tangible _____s and intangible _____s.
   a. Income   b. Asset
   c. Accounts payable   d. EBITDA

19. The term _____ has three unrelated technical definitions, and is also used in a variety of non-technical ways.

   - In financial economics, it refers to any asset used to make money, as opposed to assets used for personal enjoyment or consumption. This is an important distinction because two people can disagree sharply about the value of personal assets, one person might think a sports car is more valuable than a pickup truck, another person might have the opposite taste. But if an asset is held for the purpose of making money, taste has nothing to do with it, only differences of opinion about how much money the asset will produce. With the further assumption that people agree on the probability distribution of future cash flows, it is possible to have an objective _____ pricing model. Even without the assumption of agreement, it is possible to set rational limits on _____ value.
   - In governmental accounting, it is defined as any asset used in operations with an initial useful life extending beyond one reporting period. Generally, government managers have a 'stewardship' duty to maintain _____s under their control. See International Public Sector Accounting Standards for details.
   - In US tax accounting, it is defined as any property other than a list of exceptions. The main exceptions are anything held for sale, and any real estate or depreciable property used in business. Almost everything you own and use for personal purposes, pleasure or investment is a _____. If something is a _____ for tax purposes, gains or losses on sale or disposition are capital gains or capital losses. For individuals, however, capital losses on property held for personal use are generally not deductible. See the IRS publication Tax Facts about Capital Gains and Losses for details.

A well-known financial accounting textbook advises that the term be avoided except in tax accounting because it is used in so many different senses, not all of them well-defined. For example it is often used as a synonym for fixed assets or for investments in securities.

A common non-technical usage occurs when people ask that employees or the environment or something else be treated as a _____.

   a. Solvency   b. Settlement date
   c. Political risk   d. Capital Asset

Chapter 10. Valuation: The Entrepreneur's Perspective

20. In finance, the _____ is used to determine a theoretically appropriate required rate of return of an asset, if that asset is to be added to an already well-diversified portfolio, given that asset's non-diversifiable risk. The model takes into account the asset's sensitivity to non-diversifiable risk (also known as systemic risk or market risk), often represented by the quantity beta (β) in the financial industry, as well as the expected return of the market and the expected return of a theoretical risk-free asset.

The model was introduced by Jack Treynor (1961, 1962), William Sharpe (1964), John Lintner (1965a,b) and Jan Mossin (1966) independently, building on the earlier work of Harry Markowitz on diversification and modern portfolio theory.

   a. Random walk hypothesis
   b. Hull-White model
   c. Cox-Ingersoll-Ross model
   d. Capital Asset Pricing Model

21. A _____ is a portfolio consisting of a weighted sum of every asset in the market, with weights in the proportions that they exist in the market (with the necessary assumption that these assets are infinitely divisible.)

Neha Tyagi's critique (1977) states that this is only a theoretical concept, as to create a _____ for investment purposes in practice would necessarily include every single possible available asset, including real estate, precious metals, stamp collections, jewelry, and anything with any worth, as the theoretical market being referred to would be the world market. As a result, proxies for the market are used in practice by investors.

   a. Market price
   b. Delta neutral
   c. Central Securities Depository
   d. Market portfolio

22. The _____ is the guaranteed payoff at which a person is 'indifferent' between accepting the guaranteed payoff and a higher but uncertain payoff. (It is the amount of the higher payout minus the risk premium).

   a. Certainty equivalent
   b. 4-4-5 Calendar
   c. 7-Eleven
   d. 529 plan

23. In finance, _____, also known as return on investment is the ratio of money gained or lost on an investment relative to the amount of money invested. The amount of money gained or lost may be referred to as interest, profit/loss, gain/loss, or net income/loss. The money invested may be referred to as the asset, capital, principal, or the cost basis of the investment.

   a. Rate of return
   b. Stock or scrip dividends
   c. Composiition of Creditors
   d. Doctrine of the Proper Law

24. _____ is a form of corporation equity ownership represented in the securities. It is dangerous in comparison to preferred shares and some other investment options, in that in the event of bankruptcy, _____ investors receive their funds after preferred stockholders, bondholders, creditors, etc. On the other hand, common shares on average perform better than preferred shares or bonds over time.

   a. Stop-limit order
   b. Stock market bubble
   c. Stock split
   d. Common stock

Chapter 10. Valuation: The Entrepreneur's Perspective

25. _____ refers to the stock of skills and knowledge embodied in the ability to perform labor so as to produce economic value. Many early economic theories refer to it simply as labor, one of three factors of production, and consider it to be a fungible resource -- homogeneous and easily interchangeable. Other conceptions of labor dispense with these assumptions.

   a. Behavioral finance
   b. Human capital
   c. Market structure
   d. Mercantilism

26. _____ can be regarded as an outcome of mental processes (cognitive process) leading to the selection of a course of action among several alternatives. Every _____ process produces a final choice. The output can be an action or an opinion of choice.

   a. Decision making
   b. 4-4-5 Calendar
   c. 7-Eleven
   d. 529 plan

27. _____ are made by investors and investment managers.

Investors commonly perform investment analysis by making use of fundamental analysis, technical analysis and gut feel.

_____ are often supported by decision tools.

   a. Asset allocation
   b. Investment performance
   c. Investing online
   d. Investment decisions

28. _____ is the study of how the variation (uncertainty) in the output of a mathematical model can be apportioned, qualitatively or quantitatively, to different sources of variation in the input of a model.

In more general terms uncertainty and sensitivity analyses investigate the robustness of a study when the study includes some form of mathematical modelling. While uncertainty analysis studies the overall uncertainty in the conclusions of the study, _____ tries to identify what source of uncertainty weights more on the study's conclusions.

   a. Synthetic CDO
   b. Proxy fight
   c. Sensitivity analysis
   d. Golden parachute

29. In the most general sense, a _____ is anything that is a hindrance, or puts individuals at a disadvantage.

Before we discuss the financial terms, we should note that a _____ can also have a much more important slang meaning.

This is best described in an example.

   a. McFadden Act
   b. Liability
   c. Limited liability
   d. Covenant

Chapter 10. Valuation: The Entrepreneur's Perspective

30. _____ is a concept whereby a person's financial liability is limited to a fixed sum, most commonly the value of a person's investment in a company or partnership with _____. A shareholder in a limited company is not personally liable for any of the debts of the company, other than for the value of his investment in that company. The same is true for the members of a _____ partnership and the limited partners in a limited partnership.
   a. Personal property
   b. Sarbanes-Oxley Act
   c. Beneficial owner
   d. Limited liability

31. A _____ has elements of partnerships and corporations. In an _____ one partner is not responsible or liable for another partner's misconduct or negligence. This is an important difference from that of a limited partnership.
   a. Governmental Accounting Standards Board
   b. Limited liability partnership
   c. Citrix Systems
   d. KPMG

32. A _____ is a form of partnership similar to a general partnership, except that in addition to one or more general partners (GPs), there are one or more limited partners (_____s). It is a partnership in which only one partner is required to be a general partner.

The GPs are, in all major respects, in the same legal position as partners in a conventional firm, i.e. they have management control, share the right to use partnership property, share the profits of the firm in predefined proportions, and have joint and several liability for the debts of the partnership.

   a. Fund of funds
   b. Leverage
   c. Limited partnership
   d. Limited liability company

33. A _____ is a type of business entity in which partners (owners) share with each other the profits or losses of the business undertaking in which all have invested. _____s are often favored over corporations for taxation purposes, as the _____ structure does not generally incur a tax on profits before it is distributed to the partners (i.e. there is no dividend tax levied.) However, depending on the _____ structure and the jurisdiction in which it operates, owners of a _____ may be exposed to greater personal liability than they would as shareholders of a corporation.
   a. Clayton Antitrust Act
   b. Partnership
   c. National Securities Markets Improvement Act of 1996
   d. Fiduciary

34. In economics, _____ is a measure of the relative satisfaction from or desirability of consumption of various goods and services. Given this measure, one may speak meaningfully of increasing or decreasing _____, and thereby explain economic behavior in terms of attempts to increase one's _____. For illustrative purposes, changes in _____ are sometimes expressed in units called utils.
   a. Utility
   b. Utility function
   c. AAB
   d. A Random Walk Down Wall Street

35. A _____ is a decision support tool that uses a tree-like graph or model of decisions and their possible consequences, including chance event outcomes, resource costs, and utility. _____s are commonly used in operations research, specifically in decision analysis, to help identify a strategy most likely to reach a goal. Another use of _____s is as a descriptive means for calculating conditional probabilities.
   a. 529 plan
   b. 7-Eleven
   c. 4-4-5 Calendar
   d. Decision tree

Chapter 11. Financial Contracting with Symmetric Information

1. A '_____' is a 'Charge' that is paid to obtain the right to delay a payment. Essentially, the payer purchases the right to make a given payment in the future instead of in the Present. The '_____', or 'Charge' that must be paid to delay the payment, is simply the difference between what the payment amount would be if it were paid in the present and what the payment amount would be paid if it were paid in the future.
   - a. Risk aversion
   - b. Value at risk
   - c. Discount
   - d. Risk modeling

2. The _____ is an interest rate a central bank charges depository institutions that borrow reserves from it.

   The term _____ has two meanings:

   - the same as interest rate; the term 'discount' does not refer to the meaning of the word, but to the purpose of using the quantity, such as computations of present value, e.g. net present value / discounted cash flow

   - the annual effective _____, which is the annual interest divided by the capital including that interest; this rate is lower than the interest rate; it corresponds to using the value after a year as the nominal value, and seeing the initial value as the nominal value minus a discount; it is used for Treasury Bills and similar financial instruments

   The annual effective _____ is the annual interest divided by the capital including that interest, which is the interest rate divided by 100% plus the interest rate. It is the annual discount factor to be applied to the future cash flow, to find the discount, subtracted from a future value to find the value one year earlier.

   For example, suppose there is a government bond that sells for $95 and pays $100 in a year's time.

   - a. Discount Rate
   - b. Fisher equation
   - c. Black-Scholes
   - d. Stochastic volatility

3. The _____ of 1974 (Pub.L. 93-406, 88 Stat. 829, enacted September 2, 1974) is an American federal statute that establishes minimum standards for pension plans in private industry and provides for extensive rules on the federal income tax effects of transactions associated with employee benefit plans.
   - a. Articles of Partnership
   - b. Express warranty
   - c. Employee Retirement Income Security Act
   - d. Expedited Funds Availability Act

4. _____, refers to consumption opportunity gained by an entity within a specified time frame, which is generally expressed in monetary terms. However, for households and individuals, '_____ is the sum of all the wages, salaries, profits, interests payments, rents and other forms of earnings received... in a given period of time.' For firms, _____ generally refers to net-profit: what remains of revenue after expenses have been subtracted.
   - a. OIBDA
   - b. Annual report
   - c. Accrual
   - d. Income

5. An _____ is a contract written by a seller that conveys to the buyer the right -- but not the obligation -- to buy (in the case of a call _____) or to sell (in the case of a put _____) a particular asset, such as a piece of property such as, among others, a futures contract. In return for granting the _____, the seller collects a payment (the premium) from the buyer.

For example, buying a call _____ provides the right to buy a specified quantity of a security at a set strike price at some time on or before expiration, while buying a put _____ provides the right to sell.

a. AT'T Mobility LLC
b. Option
c. Amortization
d. Annuity

6. A _____ is a fungible, negotiable instrument representing financial value. They are broadly categorized into debt securities (such as banknotes, bonds and debentures), and equity securities; e.g., common stocks. The company or other entity issuing the _____ is called the issuer.

a. Securities lending
b. Tracking stock
c. Book entry
d. Security

7. _____ is a type of private equity capital typically provided to early-stage, high-potential, growth companies in the interest of generating a return through an eventual realization event such as an IPO or trade sale of the company. _____ investments are generally made as cash in exchange for shares in the invested company. It is typical for _____ investors to identify and back companies in high technology industries such as biotechnology and ICT.

a. Probability distribution
b. Venture Capital
c. Treasury Inflation-Protected Securities
d. Tail risk

8. A _____ is a corporation in the United States that, for Federal income tax purposes, is taxed under 26 U.S.C. Â§ 11 and Subchapter C (26 U.S.C. Â§ 11 and Subchapter C (26 U.S.C. Â§ 301 et seq.) of Chapter 1 of the Internal Revenue Code. Most major companies (and many smaller companies) are treated as _____ for Federal income tax purposes.

The income of a _____ is taxed, whereas the income of an S corporation (with a few exceptions) is not taxed under the Federal income tax laws. The income, or loss, is applied, Pro Rata, to each Shareholder and appears on their tax return as Schedule E income/(loss).

a. 4-4-5 Calendar
b. 7-Eleven
c. C corporation
d. 529 plan

9. An _____ is a corporation that makes a valid election to be taxed under Subchapter S of Chapter 1 of the Internal Revenue Code.

In general, _____s do not pay any income taxes. Instead, the corporation's income or losses are divided among and passed through to its shareholders.

a. 4-4-5 Calendar
b. 529 plan
c. S corporation
d. 7-Eleven

10. The institution most often referenced by the word '_____' is a public or publicly traded _____, the shares of which are traded on a public stock exchange (e.g., the New York Stock Exchange or Nasdaq in the United States) where shares of stock of _____s are bought and sold by and to the general public. Most of the largest businesses in the world are publicly traded _____s. However, the majority of _____s are said to be closely held, privately held or close _____s, meaning that no ready market exists for the trading of shares.

a. Federal Home Loan Mortgage Corporation
b. Corporation
c. Protect
d. Depository Trust Company

11. In economics, business, and accounting, a _____ is the value of money that has been used up to produce something, and hence is not available for use anymore. In business, the _____ may be one of acquisition, in which case the amount of money expended to acquire it is counted as _____. In this case, money is the input that is gone in order to acquire the thing.
   a. Sliding scale fees
   b. Cost
   c. Fixed costs
   d. Marginal cost

12. The _____ is an expected return that the provider of capital plans to earn on their investment.

Capital (money) used for funding a business should earn returns for the capital providers who risk their capital. For an investment to be worthwhile, the expected return on capital must be greater than the _____.

   a. Capital intensity
   b. Weighted average cost of capital
   c. Cost of capital
   d. 4-4-5 Calendar

13. _____ or financing is to provide capital (funds), which means money for a project, a person, a business or any other private or public institutions.

Those funds can be allocated for either short term or long term purposes. The health fund is a new way of _____ private healthcare centers.

   a. Synthetic CDO
   b. Product life cycle
   c. Funding
   d. Proxy fight

14. An _____ is a company whose main business is holding securities of other companies purely for investment purposes. The _____ invests money on behalf of its shareholders who in turn share in the profits and losses.
   a. Investment Company
   b. Unit investment trust
   c. AAB
   d. A Random Walk Down Wall Street

15. _____ or net present worth (NPW) is defined as the total present value (PV) of a time series of cash flows. It is a standard method for using the time value of money to appraise long-term projects. Used for capital budgeting, and widely throughout economics, it measures the excess or shortfall of cash flows, in present value terms, once financing charges are met.
   a. Negative gearing
   b. Net present value
   c. Tax shield
   d. Present value of costs

16. _____ is the value on a given date of a future payment or series of future payments, discounted to reflect the time value of money and other factors such as investment risk. _____ calculations are widely used in business and economics to provide a means to compare cash flows at different times on a meaningful 'like to like' basis.

The most commonly applied model of the time value of money is compound interest.

Chapter 11. Financial Contracting with Symmetric Information 85

a. Net present value
c. Negative gearing
b. Present value of benefits
d. Present value

17. In business and accounting, _____s are everything of value that is owned by a person or company. The balance sheet of a firm records the monetary value of the _____s owned by the firm. The two major _____ classes are tangible _____s and intangible _____s.
   a. Income
   c. Accounts payable
   b. EBITDA
   d. Asset

18. In finance, _____ is the process of estimating the potential market value of a financial asset or liability. they can be done on assets (for example, investments in marketable securities such as stocks, options, business enterprises, or intangible assets such as patents and trademarks) or on liabilities (e.g., Bonds issued by a company.) _____s are required in many contexts including investment analysis, capital budgeting, merger and acquisition transactions, financial reporting, taxable events to determine the proper tax liability, and in litigation.
   a. Margin
   c. Share
   b. Procter ' Gamble
   d. Valuation

19. The term _____ has three unrelated technical definitions, and is also used in a variety of non-technical ways.

   - In financial economics, it refers to any asset used to make money, as opposed to assets used for personal enjoyment or consumption. This is an important distinction because two people can disagree sharply about the value of personal assets, one person might think a sports car is more valuable than a pickup truck, another person might have the opposite taste. But if an asset is held for the purpose of making money, taste has nothing to do with it, only differences of opinion about how much money the asset will produce. With the further assumption that people agree on the probability distribution of future cash flows, it is possible to have an objective _____ pricing model. Even without the assumption of agreement, it is possible to set rational limits on _____ value.
   - In governmental accounting, it is defined as any asset used in operations with an initial useful life extending beyond one reporting period. Generally, government managers have a 'stewardship' duty to maintain _____s under their control. See International Public Sector Accounting Standards for details.
   - In US tax accounting, it is defined as any property other than a list of exceptions. The main exceptions are anything held for sale, and any real estate or depreciable property used in business. Almost everything you own and use for personal purposes, pleasure or investment is a _____. If something is a _____ for tax purposes, gains or losses on sale or disposition are capital gains or capital losses. For individuals, however, capital losses on property held for personal use are generally not deductible. See the IRS publication Tax Facts about Capital Gains and Losses for details.

A well-known financial accounting textbook advises that the term be avoided except in tax accounting because it is used in so many different senses, not all of them well-defined. For example it is often used as a synonym for fixed assets or for investments in securities.

A common non-technical usage occurs when people ask that employees or the environment or something else be treated as a _____.

a. Solvency
c. Political risk
b. Settlement date
d. Capital Asset

Chapter 11. Financial Contracting with Symmetric Information

20. In finance, the _____ is used to determine a theoretically appropriate required rate of return of an asset, if that asset is to be added to an already well-diversified portfolio, given that asset's non-diversifiable risk. The model takes into account the asset's sensitivity to non-diversifiable risk (also known as systemic risk or market risk), often represented by the quantity beta (β) in the financial industry, as well as the expected return of the market and the expected return of a theoretical risk-free asset.

The model was introduced by Jack Treynor (1961, 1962), William Sharpe (1964), John Lintner (1965a,b) and Jan Mossin (1966) independently, building on the earlier work of Harry Markowitz on diversification and modern portfolio theory.

- a. Random walk hypothesis
- b. Hull-White model
- c. Capital Asset Pricing Model
- d. Cox-Ingersoll-Ross model

21. _____ is the price at which an asset would trade in a competitive Walrasian auction setting. _____ is often used interchangeably with open _____, fair value or fair _____, although these terms have distinct definitions in different standards, and may differ in some circumstances.

International Valuation Standards defines _____ as 'the estimated amount for which a property should exchange on the date of valuation between a willing buyer and a willing seller in an arm'e;s-length transaction after proper marketing wherein the parties had each acted knowledgeably, prudently, and without compulsion.'

_____ is a concept distinct from market price, which is 'e;the price at which one can transact'e;, while _____ is 'e;the true underlying value'e; according to theoretical standards.

- a. T-Model
- b. Market value
- c. Wrap account
- d. Debt restructuring

22. _____ can be regarded as an outcome of mental processes (cognitive process) leading to the selection of a course of action among several alternatives. Every _____ process produces a final choice. The output can be an action or an opinion of choice.

- a. 7-Eleven
- b. 4-4-5 Calendar
- c. 529 plan
- d. Decision making

23. In the most general sense, a _____ is anything that is a hindrance, or puts individuals at a disadvantage.

Before we discuss the financial terms, we should note that a _____ can also have a much more important slang meaning.

This is best described in an example.

- a. Liability
- b. Covenant
- c. Limited liability
- d. McFadden Act

24. _____ is a concept whereby a person's financial liability is limited to a fixed sum, most commonly the value of a person's investment in a company or partnership with _____. A shareholder in a limited company is not personally liable for any of the debts of the company, other than for the value of his investment in that company. The same is true for the members of a _____ partnership and the limited partners in a limited partnership.
  a. Beneficial owner
  b. Personal property
  c. Sarbanes-Oxley Act
  d. Limited liability

25. A _____ has elements of partnerships and corporations. In an _____ one partner is not responsible or liable for another partner's misconduct or negligence. This is an important difference from that of a limited partnership.
  a. Governmental Accounting Standards Board
  b. Limited liability partnership
  c. KPMG
  d. Citrix Systems

26. A _____ is a form of partnership similar to a general partnership, except that in addition to one or more general partners (GPs), there are one or more limited partners (_____s). It is a partnership in which only one partner is required to be a general partner.

The GPs are, in all major respects, in the same legal position as partners in a conventional firm, i.e. they have management control, share the right to use partnership property, share the profits of the firm in predefined proportions, and have joint and several liability for the debts of the partnership.

  a. Leverage
  b. Fund of funds
  c. Limited liability company
  d. Limited partnership

27. A _____ is a type of business entity in which partners (owners) share with each other the profits or losses of the business undertaking in which all have invested. _____s are often favored over corporations for taxation purposes, as the _____ structure does not generally incur a tax on profits before it is distributed to the partners (i.e. there is no dividend tax levied.) However, depending on the _____ structure and the jurisdiction in which it operates, owners of a _____ may be exposed to greater personal liability than they would as shareholders of a corporation.
  a. Clayton Antitrust Act
  b. Fiduciary
  c. National Securities Markets Improvement Act of 1996
  d. Partnership

28. _____ is an organization's process of defining its strategy and making decisions on allocating its resources to pursue this strategy, including its capital and people. Various business analysis techniques can be used in _____, including SWOT analysis (Strengths, Weaknesses, Opportunities, and Threats) and PEST analysis (Political, Economic, Social, and Technological analysis) or STEER analysis involving Socio-cultural, Technological, Economic, Ecological, and Regulatory factors and EPISTEL (Environment, Political, Informatic, Social, Technological, Economic and Legal)

_____ is the formal consideration of an organization's future course. All _____ deals with at least one of three key questions:

1. 'What do we do?'
2. 'For whom do we do it?'
3. 'How do we excel?'

In business _____, the third question is better phrased 'How can we beat or avoid competition?'. (Bradford and Duncan, page 1.)

a. 4-4-5 Calendar
b. 7-Eleven
c. 529 plan
d. Strategic planning

29. An _____ or angel is an affluent individual who provides capital for a business start-up, usually in exchange for convertible debt or ownership equity. A small but increasing number of _____s organize themselves into angel groups or angel networks to share research and pool their investment capital.

Angels typically invest their own funds, unlike venture capitalists, who manage the pooled money of others in a professionally-managed fund.

a. A Random Walk Down Wall Street
b. AAB
c. ABN Amro
d. Angel investor

30. In the United States, a _____ is an offering of securities that are not registered with the Securities and Exchange Commission (SEC.) Such offerings exploit an exemption offered by the Securities Act of 1933 that comes with several restrictions, including a prohibition against general solicitation. This exemption allows companies to avoid quarterly reporting requirements and many of the legal liabilities associated with the Sarbanes-Oxley Act.

a. 529 plan
b. 4-4-5 Calendar
c. 7-Eleven
d. Private placement

Chapter 12. Dealing with Information and Incentive Problems

1. A '_____' is a 'Charge' that is paid to obtain the right to delay a payment. Essentially, the payer purchases the right to make a given payment in the future instead of in the Present. The '_____', or 'Charge' that must be paid to delay the payment, is simply the difference between what the payment amount would be if it were paid in the present and what the payment amount would be paid if it were paid in the future.

   a. Value at risk
   b. Risk modeling
   c. Discount
   d. Risk aversion

2. The _____ is an interest rate a central bank charges depository institutions that borrow reserves from it.

The term _____ has two meanings:

- the same as interest rate; the term 'discount' does not refer to the meaning of the word, but to the purpose of using the quantity, such as computations of present value, e.g. net present value / discounted cash flow

- the annual effective _____, which is the annual interest divided by the capital including that interest; this rate is lower than the interest rate; it corresponds to using the value after a year as the nominal value, and seeing the initial value as the nominal value minus a discount; it is used for Treasury Bills and similar financial instruments

The annual effective _____ is the annual interest divided by the capital including that interest, which is the interest rate divided by 100% plus the interest rate. It is the annual discount factor to be applied to the future cash flow, to find the discount, subtracted from a future value to find the value one year earlier.

For example, suppose there is a government bond that sells for $95 and pays $100 in a year's time.

   a. Fisher equation
   b. Discount Rate
   c. Black-Scholes
   d. Stochastic volatility

3. A _____ is a fungible, negotiable instrument representing financial value. They are broadly categorized into debt securities (such as banknotes, bonds and debentures), and equity securities; e.g., common stocks. The company or other entity issuing the _____ is called the issuer.

   a. Book entry
   b. Security
   c. Securities lending
   d. Tracking stock

4. The U.S. _____ is an independent agency of the United States government which holds primary responsibility for enforcing the federal securities laws and regulating the securities industry, the nation's stock and options exchanges, and other electronic securities markets. The SEC was created by section 4 of the SEC of 1934 (now codified as 15 U.S.C. § 78d and commonly referred to as the 1934 Act.)

   a. 7-Eleven
   b. 529 plan
   c. 4-4-5 Calendar
   d. Securities and Exchange Commission

5. _____ is a type of private equity capital typically provided to early-stage, high-potential, growth companies in the interest of generating a return through an eventual realization event such as an IPO or trade sale of the company. _____ investments are generally made as cash in exchange for shares in the invested company. It is typical for _____ investors to identify and back companies in high technology industries such as biotechnology and ICT.

Chapter 12. Dealing with Information and Incentive Problems

a. Tail risk
b. Probability distribution
c. Treasury Inflation-Protected Securities
d. Venture Capital

6. A _____ is an exchange of promises between two or more parties to do an act which is enforceable in a court of law. It is where an unqualified offer meets a qualified acceptance and the parties reach Consensus ad Idem. The parties must have the necessary capacity to _____ and the _____ must not be either trifling, indeterminate, impossible or illegal.

a. 529 plan
b. 7-Eleven
c. 4-4-5 Calendar
d. Contract

7. In economics, business, and accounting, a _____ is the value of money that has been used up to produce something, and hence is not available for use anymore. In business, the _____ may be one of acquisition, in which case the amount of money expended to acquire it is counted as _____. In this case, money is the input that is gone in order to acquire the thing.

a. Marginal cost
b. Fixed costs
c. Sliding scale fees
d. Cost

8. A _____ is a corporation in the United States that, for Federal income tax purposes, is taxed under 26 U.S.C. Â§ 11 and Subchapter C (26 U.S.C. Â§ 11 and Subchapter C (26 U.S.C. Â§ 301 et seq.) of Chapter 1 of the Internal Revenue Code. Most major companies (and many smaller companies) are treated as _____ for Federal income tax purposes.

The income of a _____ is taxed, whereas the income of an S corporation (with a few exceptions) is not taxed under the Federal income tax laws. The income, or loss, is applied, Pro Rata, to each Shareholder and appears on their tax return as Schedule E income/(loss).

a. 529 plan
b. 4-4-5 Calendar
c. 7-Eleven
d. C corporation

9. The _____ of 1974 (Pub.L. 93-406, 88 Stat. 829, enacted September 2, 1974) is an American federal statute that establishes minimum standards for pension plans in private industry and provides for extensive rules on the federal income tax effects of transactions associated with employee benefit plans.

a. Articles of Partnership
b. Express warranty
c. Expedited Funds Availability Act
d. Employee Retirement Income Security Act

10. _____, refers to consumption opportunity gained by an entity within a specified time frame, which is generally expressed in monetary terms. However, for households and individuals, '_____ is the sum of all the wages, salaries, profits, interests payments, rents and other forms of earnings received... in a given period of time.' For firms, _____ generally refers to net-profit: what remains of revenue after expenses have been subtracted.

a. Annual report
b. Accrual
c. OIBDA
d. Income

11. An _____ is a corporation that makes a valid election to be taxed under Subchapter S of Chapter 1 of the Internal Revenue Code.

In general, _____s do not pay any income taxes. Instead, the corporation's income or losses are divided among and passed through to its shareholders.

Chapter 12. Dealing with Information and Incentive Problems

a. 4-4-5 Calendar
c. S corporation
b. 7-Eleven
d. 529 plan

12. The institution most often referenced by the word '_____' is a public or publicly traded _____, the shares of which are traded on a public stock exchange (e.g., the New York Stock Exchange or Nasdaq in the United States) where shares of stock of _____s are bought and sold by and to the general public. Most of the largest businesses in the world are publicly traded _____s. However, the majority of _____s are said to be closely held, privately held or close _____s, meaning that no ready market exists for the trading of shares.

a. Protect
c. Depository Trust Company
b. Federal Home Loan Mortgage Corporation
d. Corporation

13. The _____ is an expected return that the provider of capital plans to earn on their investment.

Capital (money) used for funding a business should earn returns for the capital providers who risk their capital. For an investment to be worthwhile, the expected return on capital must be greater than the _____.

a. Capital intensity
c. 4-4-5 Calendar
b. Cost of capital
d. Weighted average cost of capital

14. In business and accounting, _____s are everything of value that is owned by a person or company. The balance sheet of a firm records the monetary value of the _____s owned by the firm. The two major _____ classes are tangible _____s and intangible _____s.

a. EBITDA
c. Income
b. Accounts payable
d. Asset

15. _____, is when a company issues common stock or shares to the public for the first time. They are often issued by smaller, younger companies seeking capital to expand, but can also be done by large privately-owned companies looking to become publicly traded.

In an _____ the issuer may obtain the assistance of an underwriting firm, which helps it determine what type of security to issue (common or preferred), best offering price and time to bring it to market.

a. Asian Financial Crisis
c. Interest
b. Insolvency
d. Initial public offering

16. An _____ is a contract written by a seller that conveys to the buyer the right -- but not the obligation -- to buy (in the case of a call _____) or to sell (in the case of a put _____) a particular asset, such as a piece of property such as, among others, a futures contract. In return for granting the _____, the seller collects a payment (the premium) from the buyer.

For example, buying a call _____ provides the right to buy a specified quantity of a security at a set strike price at some time on or before expiration, while buying a put _____ provides the right to sell.

a. AT'T Mobility LLC
c. Amortization
b. Option
d. Annuity

Chapter 12. Dealing with Information and Incentive Problems

17. _____ are costs incurred on the purchase of land, buildings, construction and equipment to be used in the production of goods or the rendering of services. In other words, the total cost needed to bring a project to a commercially operable status. However, _____ are not limited to the initial construction of a factory or other business.
   a. Capital outflow
   b. Trade-off
   c. Defined contribution plan
   d. Capital costs

18. _____ is that which is owed; usually referencing assets owed, but the term can cover other obligations. In the case of assets, _____ is a means of using future purchasing power in the present before a summation has been earned. Some companies and corporations use _____ as a part of their overall corporate finance strategy.
   a. Credit cycle
   b. Partial Payment
   c. Cross-collateralization
   d. Debt

19. _____ or financing is to provide capital (funds), which means money for a project, a person, a business or any other private or public institutions.

Those funds can be allocated for either short term or long term purposes. The health fund is a new way of _____ private healthcare centers.

   a. Synthetic CDO
   b. Product life cycle
   c. Proxy fight
   d. Funding

20. _____ is a form of corporation equity ownership represented in the securities. It is dangerous in comparison to preferred shares and some other investment options, in that in the event of bankruptcy, _____ investors receive their funds after preferred stockholders, bondholders, creditors, etc. On the other hand, common shares on average perform better than preferred shares or bonds over time.
   a. Stock split
   b. Stop-limit order
   c. Stock market bubble
   d. Common stock

21. _____ is the price at which an asset would trade in a competitive Walrasian auction setting. _____ is often used interchangeably with open _____, fair value or fair _____, although these terms have distinct definitions in different standards, and may differ in some circumstances.

International Valuation Standards defines _____ as 'the estimated amount for which a property should exchange on the date of valuation between a willing buyer and a willing seller in an arm'e;s-length transaction after proper marketing wherein the parties had each acted knowledgeably, prudently, and without compulsion.'

_____ is a concept distinct from market price, which is 'e;the price at which one can transact'e;, while _____ is 'e;the true underlying value'e; according to theoretical standards.

   a. T-Model
   b. Debt restructuring
   c. Wrap account
   d. Market value

22. In the most general sense, a _____ is anything that is a hindrance, or puts individuals at a disadvantage.

Chapter 12. Dealing with Information and Incentive Problems

Before we discuss the financial terms, we should note that a _____ can also have a much more important slang meaning.

This is best described in an example.

a. Liability
b. Limited liability
c. Covenant
d. McFadden Act

23. _____ is a concept whereby a person's financial liability is limited to a fixed sum, most commonly the value of a person's investment in a company or partnership with _____. A shareholder in a limited company is not personally liable for any of the debts of the company, other than for the value of his investment in that company. The same is true for the members of a _____ partnership and the limited partners in a limited partnership.

a. Limited liability
b. Personal property
c. Beneficial owner
d. Sarbanes-Oxley Act

24. A _____ has elements of partnerships and corporations. In an _____ one partner is not responsible or liable for another partner's misconduct or negligence. This is an important difference from that of a limited partnership.

a. Governmental Accounting Standards Board
b. Citrix Systems
c. KPMG
d. Limited liability partnership

25. A _____ is a form of partnership similar to a general partnership, except that in addition to one or more general partners (GPs), there are one or more limited partners (_____s). It is a partnership in which only one partner is required to be a general partner.

The GPs are, in all major respects, in the same legal position as partners in a conventional firm, i.e. they have management control, share the right to use partnership property, share the profits of the firm in predefined proportions, and have joint and several liability for the debts of the partnership.

a. Fund of funds
b. Limited liability company
c. Leverage
d. Limited partnership

26. A _____ is a type of business entity in which partners (owners) share with each other the profits or losses of the business undertaking in which all have invested. _____s are often favored over corporations for taxation purposes, as the _____ structure does not generally incur a tax on profits before it is distributed to the partners (i.e. there is no dividend tax levied.) However, depending on the _____ structure and the jurisdiction in which it operates, owners of a _____ may be exposed to greater personal liability than they would as shareholders of a corporation.

a. Fiduciary
b. National Securities Markets Improvement Act of 1996
c. Clayton Antitrust Act
d. Partnership

94 Chapter 12. Dealing with Information and Incentive Problems

27. The term _____ refers to three closely related concepts:

- The _____ model is a mathematical model of the market for an equity, in which the equity's price is a stochastic process.
- The _____ PDE is a partial differential equation which (in the model) must be satisfied by the price of a derivative on the equity.
- The _____ formula is the result obtained by solving the _____ PDE for a European call option.

Fischer Black and Myron Scholes first articulated the _____ formula in their 1973 paper, 'The Pricing of Options and Corporate Liabilities.' The foundation for their research relied on work developed by scholars such as Jack L. Treynor, Paul Samuelson, A. James Boness, Sheen T. Kassouf, and Edward O. Thorp. The fundamental insight of _____ is that the option is implicitly priced if the stock is traded.

Robert C. Merton was the first to publish a paper expanding the mathematical understanding of the options pricing model and coined the term '_____' options pricing model.

a. Perpetuity
c. Modified Internal Rate of Return
b. Stochastic volatility
d. Black-Scholes

28. In finance, a _____ is a debt security, in which the authorized issuer owes the holders a debt and, depending on the terms of the _____, is obliged to pay interest (the coupon) and/or to repay the principal at a later date, termed maturity.

Thus a _____ is a loan: the issuer is the borrower, the _____ holder is the lender, and the coupon is the interest. _____s provide the borrower with external funds to finance long-term investments, or, in the case of government _____s, to finance current expenditure.

a. Puttable bond
c. Catastrophe bonds
b. Convertible bond
d. Bond

29. In economics and contract theory, _____ deals with the study of decisions in transactions where one party has more or better information than the other. This creates an imbalance of power in transactions which can sometimes cause the transactions to go awry. Examples of this problem are adverse selection and moral hazard.

a. ABN Amro
c. A Random Walk Down Wall Street
b. AAB
d. Information asymmetry

30. In finance, _____ is the process of estimating the potential market value of a financial asset or liability. they can be done on assets (for example, investments in marketable securities such as stocks, options, business enterprises, or intangible assets such as patents and trademarks) or on liabilities (e.g., Bonds issued by a company.) _____s are required in many contexts including investment analysis, capital budgeting, merger and acquisition transactions, financial reporting, taxable events to determine the proper tax liability, and in litigation.

a. Share
c. Procter ' Gamble
b. Margin
d. Valuation

Chapter 12. Dealing with Information and Incentive Problems 95

31. The term _____ has three unrelated technical definitions, and is also used in a variety of non-technical ways.

- In financial economics, it refers to any asset used to make money, as opposed to assets used for personal enjoyment or consumption. This is an important distinction because two people can disagree sharply about the value of personal assets, one person might think a sports car is more valuable than a pickup truck, another person might have the opposite taste. But if an asset is held for the purpose of making money, taste has nothing to do with it, only differences of opinion about how much money the asset will produce. With the further assumption that people agree on the probability distribution of future cash flows, it is possible to have an objective _____ pricing model. Even without the assumption of agreement, it is possible to set rational limits on _____ value.
- In governmental accounting, it is defined as any asset used in operations with an initial useful life extending beyond one reporting period. Generally, government managers have a 'stewardship' duty to maintain _____s under their control. See International Public Sector Accounting Standards for details.
- In US tax accounting, it is defined as any property other than a list of exceptions. The main exceptions are anything held for sale, and any real estate or depreciable property used in business. Almost everything you own and use for personal purposes, pleasure or investment is a _____. If something is a _____ for tax purposes, gains or losses on sale or disposition are capital gains or capital losses. For individuals, however, capital losses on property held for personal use are generally not deductible. See the IRS publication Tax Facts about Capital Gains and Losses for details.

A well-known financial accounting textbook advises that the term be avoided except in tax accounting because it is used in so many different senses, not all of them well-defined. For example it is often used as a synonym for fixed assets or for investments in securities.

A common non-technical usage occurs when people ask that employees or the environment or something else be treated as a _____.

a. Solvency
c. Settlement date
b. Capital Asset
d. Political risk

32. In finance, the _____ is used to determine a theoretically appropriate required rate of return of an asset, if that asset is to be added to an already well-diversified portfolio, given that asset's non-diversifiable risk. The model takes into account the asset's sensitivity to non-diversifiable risk (also known as systemic risk or market risk), often represented by the quantity beta (β) in the financial industry, as well as the expected return of the market and the expected return of a theoretical risk-free asset.

The model was introduced by Jack Treynor (1961, 1962), William Sharpe (1964), John Lintner (1965a,b) and Jan Mossin (1966) independently, building on the earlier work of Harry Markowitz on diversification and modern portfolio theory.

a. Random walk hypothesis
c. Cox-Ingersoll-Ross model
b. Hull-White model
d. Capital Asset Pricing Model

33. The phrase _____ refers to the aspect of corporate strategy, corporate finance and management dealing with the buying, selling and combining of different companies that can aid, finance, or help a growing company in a given industry grow rapidly without having to create another business entity.

Chapter 12. Dealing with Information and Incentive Problems

An acquisition, also known as a takeover, is the buying of one company (the 'target') by another. An acquisition may be friendly or hostile.

a. 529 plan
c. 4-4-5 Calendar
b. 7-Eleven
d. Mergers and acquisitions

34. In financial accounting, _____s are precautions for which the amount or probability of occurrence are not known. Typical examples are _____s for warranty costs and _____ for taxes the term reserve is used instead of term _____; such a use, however, is inconsistent with the terminology suggested by International Accounting Standards Board.

a. Petty cash
c. Money measurement concept
b. Momentum Accounting and Triple-Entry Bookkeeping
d. Provision

35. An _____ is a company whose main business is holding securities of other companies purely for investment purposes. The _____ invests money on behalf of its shareholders who in turn share in the profits and losses.

a. Investment Company
c. Unit investment trust
b. A Random Walk Down Wall Street
d. AAB

36. _____ is a term used for a number of concepts involving either the performance of an investigation of a business or person, or the performance of an act with a certain standard of care. It can be a legal obligation, but the term will more commonly apply to voluntary investigations. A common example of _____ in various industries is the process through which a potential acquirer evaluates a target company or its assets for acquisition.

a. Due diligence
c. Bond indenture
b. Down payment
d. Quiet period

37. The _____ is the market for securities, where companies and governments can raise longterm funds. The _____ includes the stock market and the bond market. Financial regulators, such as the U.S. Securities and Exchange Commission, oversee the _____s in their designated countries to ensure that investors are protected against fraud.

a. Spot rate
c. Forward market
b. Delta neutral
d. Capital market

38. The _____ or Venture Capital Method is a valuation method often used by venture capitalists and private equity professionals that combines elements of both a multiples-based valuation and a traditional discounted cash flow (DCF.) The method is particularly useful in valuing high-growth companies. Many practitioners feel that the method is better than a straight multiples method for valuing high-growth companies because high-growth companies do not have significant current financial results.

a. Sinking fund
c. Consumer basket
b. First Chicago method
d. Risk-return spectrum

39. _____ can be regarded as an outcome of mental processes (cognitive process) leading to the selection of a course of action among several alternatives. Every _____ process produces a final choice. The output can be an action or an opinion of choice.

a. 7-Eleven
c. 529 plan
b. 4-4-5 Calendar
d. Decision making

Chapter 13. Financial Contracting

1. A '_____' is a 'Charge' that is paid to obtain the right to delay a payment. Essentially, the payer purchases the right to make a given payment in the future instead of in the Present. The '_____', or 'Charge' that must be paid to delay the payment, is simply the difference between what the payment amount would be if it were paid in the present and what the payment amount would be paid if it were paid in the future.

   a. Value at risk   b. Risk modeling
   c. Risk aversion   d. Discount

2. The _____ is an interest rate a central bank charges depository institutions that borrow reserves from it.

The term _____ has two meanings:

- the same as interest rate; the term 'discount' does not refer to the meaning of the word, but to the purpose of using the quantity, such as computations of present value, e.g. net present value / discounted cash flow

- the annual effective _____, which is the annual interest divided by the capital including that interest; this rate is lower than the interest rate; it corresponds to using the value after a year as the nominal value, and seeing the initial value as the nominal value minus a discount; it is used for Treasury Bills and similar financial instruments

The annual effective _____ is the annual interest divided by the capital including that interest, which is the interest rate divided by 100% plus the interest rate. It is the annual discount factor to be applied to the future cash flow, to find the discount, subtracted from a future value to find the value one year earlier.

For example, suppose there is a government bond that sells for $95 and pays $100 in a year's time.

   a. Black-Scholes   b. Fisher equation
   c. Stochastic volatility   d. Discount Rate

3. _____, is when a company issues common stock or shares to the public for the first time. They are often issued by smaller, younger companies seeking capital to expand, but can also be done by large privately-owned companies looking to become publicly traded.

In an _____ the issuer may obtain the assistance of an underwriting firm, which helps it determine what type of security to issue (common or preferred), best offering price and time to bring it to market.

   a. Interest   b. Initial public offering
   c. Insolvency   d. Asian Financial Crisis

4. _____ is a type of private equity capital typically provided to early-stage, high-potential, growth companies in the interest of generating a return through an eventual realization event such as an IPO or trade sale of the company. _____ investments are generally made as cash in exchange for shares in the invested company. It is typical for _____ investors to identify and back companies in high technology industries such as biotechnology and ICT.

   a. Tail risk   b. Treasury Inflation-Protected Securities
   c. Probability distribution   d. Venture Capital

Chapter 13. Financial Contracting

5. A _____ is an exchange of promises between two or more parties to do an act which is enforceable in a court of law. It is where an unqualified offer meets a qualified acceptance and the parties reach Consensus ad Idem. The parties must have the necessary capacity to _____ and the _____ must not be either trifling, indeterminate, impossible or illegal.
   a. 529 plan
   b. Contract
   c. 4-4-5 Calendar
   d. 7-Eleven

6. _____ or financing is to provide capital (funds), which means money for a project, a person, a business or any other private or public institutions.

Those funds can be allocated for either short term or long term purposes. The health fund is a new way of _____ private healthcare centers.

   a. Funding
   b. Product life cycle
   c. Proxy fight
   d. Synthetic CDO

7. In business and accounting, _____s are everything of value that is owned by a person or company. The balance sheet of a firm records the monetary value of the _____s owned by the firm. The two major _____ classes are tangible _____s and intangible _____s.
   a. Income
   b. EBITDA
   c. Accounts payable
   d. Asset

8. In finance, _____ is the process of estimating the potential market value of a financial asset or liability. they can be done on assets (for example, investments in marketable securities such as stocks, options, business enterprises, or intangible assets such as patents and trademarks) or on liabilities (e.g., Bonds issued by a company.) _____s are required in many contexts including investment analysis, capital budgeting, merger and acquisition transactions, financial reporting, taxable events to determine the proper tax liability, and in litigation.
   a. Margin
   b. Share
   c. Procter ' Gamble
   d. Valuation

9. The term _____ has three unrelated technical definitions, and is also used in a variety of non-technical ways.

- In financial economics, it refers to any asset used to make money, as opposed to assets used for personal enjoyment or consumption. This is an important distinction because two people can disagree sharply about the value of personal assets, one person might think a sports car is more valuable than a pickup truck, another person might have the opposite taste. But if an asset is held for the purpose of making money, taste has nothing to do with it, only differences of opinion about how much money the asset will produce. With the further assumption that people agree on the probability distribution of future cash flows, it is possible to have an objective _____ pricing model. Even without the assumption of agreement, it is possible to set rational limits on _____ value.
- In governmental accounting, it is defined as any asset used in operations with an initial useful life extending beyond one reporting period. Generally, government managers have a 'stewardship' duty to maintain _____s under their control. See International Public Sector Accounting Standards for details.
- In US tax accounting, it is defined as any property other than a list of exceptions. The main exceptions are anything held for sale, and any real estate or depreciable property used in business. Almost everything you own and use for personal purposes, pleasure or investment is a _____. If something is a _____ for tax purposes, gains or losses on sale or disposition are capital gains or capital losses. For individuals, however, capital losses on property held for personal use are generally not deductible. See the IRS publication Tax Facts about Capital Gains and Losses for details.

A well-known financial accounting textbook advises that the term be avoided except in tax accounting because it is used in so many different senses, not all of them well-defined. For example it is often used as a synonym for fixed assets or for investments in securities.

A common non-technical usage occurs when people ask that employees or the environment or something else be treated as a _____.

a. Settlement date
b. Solvency
c. Political risk
d. Capital Asset

10. In finance, the _____ is used to determine a theoretically appropriate required rate of return of an asset, if that asset is to be added to an already well-diversified portfolio, given that asset's non-diversifiable risk. The model takes into account the asset's sensitivity to non-diversifiable risk (also known as systemic risk or market risk), often represented by the quantity beta (β) in the financial industry, as well as the expected return of the market and the expected return of a theoretical risk-free asset.

The model was introduced by Jack Treynor (1961, 1962), William Sharpe (1964), John Lintner (1965a,b) and Jan Mossin (1966) independently, building on the earlier work of Harry Markowitz on diversification and modern portfolio theory.

a. Capital Asset Pricing Model
b. Hull-White model
c. Cox-Ingersoll-Ross model
d. Random walk hypothesis

11. An _____ is a contract written by a seller that conveys to the buyer the right -- but not the obligation -- to buy (in the case of a call _____) or to sell (in the case of a put _____) a particular asset, such as a piece of property such as, among others, a futures contract. In return for granting the _____, the seller collects a payment (the premium) from the buyer.

Chapter 13. Financial Contracting

For example, buying a call _____ provides the right to buy a specified quantity of a security at a set strike price at some time on or before expiration, while buying a put _____ provides the right to sell.

a. Annuity
b. Amortization
c. AT'T Mobility LLC
d. Option

12. The _____ of 1974 (Pub.L. 93-406, 88 Stat. 829, enacted September 2, 1974) is an American federal statute that establishes minimum standards for pension plans in private industry and provides for extensive rules on the federal income tax effects of transactions associated with employee benefit plans.

a. Express warranty
b. Expedited Funds Availability Act
c. Articles of Partnership
d. Employee Retirement Income Security Act

13. _____, refers to consumption opportunity gained by an entity within a specified time frame, which is generally expressed in monetary terms. However, for households and individuals, '_____ is the sum of all the wages, salaries, profits, interests payments, rents and other forms of earnings received... in a given period of time.' For firms, _____ generally refers to net-profit: what remains of revenue after expenses have been subtracted.

a. Annual report
b. OIBDA
c. Accrual
d. Income

14. A _____ is a fungible, negotiable instrument representing financial value. They are broadly categorized into debt securities (such as banknotes, bonds and debentures), and equity securities; e.g., common stocks. The company or other entity issuing the _____ is called the issuer.

a. Tracking stock
b. Securities lending
c. Book entry
d. Security

15. A _____ is a corporation in the United States that, for Federal income tax purposes, is taxed under 26 U.S.C. § 11 and Subchapter C (26 U.S.C. § 11 and Subchapter C (26 U.S.C. § 301 et seq.) of Chapter 1 of the Internal Revenue Code. Most major companies (and many smaller companies) are treated as _____ for Federal income tax purposes.

The income of a _____ is taxed, whereas the income of an S corporation (with a few exceptions) is not taxed under the Federal income tax laws. The income, or loss, is applied, Pro Rata, to each Shareholder and appears on their tax return as Schedule E income/(loss).

a. 7-Eleven
b. 4-4-5 Calendar
c. 529 plan
d. C corporation

16. An _____ is a corporation that makes a valid election to be taxed under Subchapter S of Chapter 1 of the Internal Revenue Code.

In general, _____s do not pay any income taxes. Instead, the corporation's income or losses are divided among and passed through to its shareholders.

a. 529 plan
b. 4-4-5 Calendar
c. 7-Eleven
d. S corporation

Chapter 13. Financial Contracting

17. The institution most often referenced by the word '_____' is a public or publicly traded _____, the shares of which are traded on a public stock exchange (e.g., the New York Stock Exchange or Nasdaq in the United States) where shares of stock of _____s are bought and sold by and to the general public. Most of the largest businesses in the world are publicly traded _____s. However, the majority of _____s are said to be closely held, privately held or close _____s, meaning that no ready market exists for the trading of shares.
   a. Federal Home Loan Mortgage Corporation
   b. Protect
   c. Depository Trust Company
   d. Corporation

18. In economics, business, and accounting, a _____ is the value of money that has been used up to produce something, and hence is not available for use anymore. In business, the _____ may be one of acquisition, in which case the amount of money expended to acquire it is counted as _____. In this case, money is the input that is gone in order to acquire the thing.
   a. Marginal cost
   b. Sliding scale fees
   c. Fixed costs
   d. Cost

19. The _____ is an expected return that the provider of capital plans to earn on their investment.

Capital (money) used for funding a business should earn returns for the capital providers who risk their capital. For an investment to be worthwhile, the expected return on capital must be greater than the _____.

   a. 4-4-5 Calendar
   b. Weighted average cost of capital
   c. Capital intensity
   d. Cost of capital

20. A _____ is a decision support tool that uses a tree-like graph or model of decisions and their possible consequences, including chance event outcomes, resource costs, and utility. _____s are commonly used in operations research, specifically in decision analysis, to help identify a strategy most likely to reach a goal. Another use of _____s is as a descriptive means for calculating conditional probabilities.
   a. 4-4-5 Calendar
   b. 7-Eleven
   c. 529 plan
   d. Decision tree

21. _____ is an organization's process of defining its strategy and making decisions on allocating its resources to pursue this strategy, including its capital and people. Various business analysis techniques can be used in _____, including SWOT analysis (Strengths, Weaknesses, Opportunities, and Threats) and PEST analysis (Political, Economic, Social, and Technological analysis) or STEER analysis involving Socio-cultural, Technological, Economic, Ecological, and Regulatory factors and EPISTEL (Environment, Political, Informatic, Social, Technological, Economic and Legal)

_____ is the formal consideration of an organization's future course. All _____ deals with at least one of three key questions:

   1. 'What do we do?'
   2. 'For whom do we do it?'
   3. 'How do we excel?'

In business _____, the third question is better phrased 'How can we beat or avoid competition?'. (Bradford and Duncan, page 1.)

Chapter 13. Financial Contracting

a. 4-4-5 Calendar
b. 529 plan
c. 7-Eleven
d. Strategic planning

22. In financial accounting, _____s are precautions for which the amount or probability of occurrence are not known. Typical examples are _____s for warranty costs and _____ for taxes the term reserve is used instead of term _____; such a use, however, is inconsistent with the terminology suggested by International Accounting Standards Board.
 a. Momentum Accounting and Triple-Entry Bookkeeping
 b. Petty cash
 c. Money measurement concept
 d. Provision

23. _____ or net present worth (NPW) is defined as the total present value (PV) of a time series of cash flows. It is a standard method for using the time value of money to appraise long-term projects. Used for capital budgeting, and widely throughout economics, it measures the excess or shortfall of cash flows, in present value terms, once financing charges are met.
 a. Tax shield
 b. Negative gearing
 c. Present value of costs
 d. Net present value

24. _____ is the value on a given date of a future payment or series of future payments, discounted to reflect the time value of money and other factors such as investment risk. _____ calculations are widely used in business and economics to provide a means to compare cash flows at different times on a meaningful 'like to like' basis.

The most commonly applied model of the time value of money is compound interest.

 a. Present value of benefits
 b. Net present value
 c. Negative gearing
 d. Present value

Chapter 14. Venture Capital

1. A '_____' is a 'Charge' that is paid to obtain the right to delay a payment. Essentially, the payer purchases the right to make a given payment in the future instead of in the Present. The '_____', or 'Charge' that must be paid to delay the payment, is simply the difference between what the payment amount would be if it were paid in the present and what the payment amount would be paid if it were paid in the future.
   a. Value at risk
   b. Risk aversion
   c. Risk modeling
   d. Discount

2. The _____ is an interest rate a central bank charges depository institutions that borrow reserves from it.

The term _____ has two meanings:

- the same as interest rate; the term 'discount' does not refer to the meaning of the word, but to the purpose of using the quantity, such as computations of present value, e.g. net present value / discounted cash flow

- the annual effective _____, which is the annual interest divided by the capital including that interest; this rate is lower than the interest rate; it corresponds to using the value after a year as the nominal value, and seeing the initial value as the nominal value minus a discount; it is used for Treasury Bills and similar financial instruments

The annual effective _____ is the annual interest divided by the capital including that interest, which is the interest rate divided by 100% plus the interest rate. It is the annual discount factor to be applied to the future cash flow, to find the discount, subtracted from a future value to find the value one year earlier.

For example, suppose there is a government bond that sells for $95 and pays $100 in a year's time.

   a. Black-Scholes
   b. Fisher equation
   c. Discount Rate
   d. Stochastic volatility

3. _____ is a type of private equity capital typically provided to early-stage, high-potential, growth companies in the interest of generating a return through an eventual realization event such as an IPO or trade sale of the company. _____ investments are generally made as cash in exchange for shares in the invested company. It is typical for _____ investors to identify and back companies in high technology industries such as biotechnology and ICT.
   a. Tail risk
   b. Probability distribution
   c. Treasury Inflation-Protected Securities
   d. Venture Capital

4. In business and accounting, _____s are everything of value that is owned by a person or company. The balance sheet of a firm records the monetary value of the _____s owned by the firm. The two major _____ classes are tangible _____s and intangible _____s.
   a. Asset
   b. Income
   c. Accounts payable
   d. EBITDA

5. In finance, _____ is the process of estimating the potential market value of a financial asset or liability. they can be done on assets (for example, investments in marketable securities such as stocks, options, business enterprises, or intangible assets such as patents and trademarks) or on liabilities (e.g., Bonds issued by a company.) _____s are required in many contexts including investment analysis, capital budgeting, merger and acquisition transactions, financial reporting, taxable events to determine the proper tax liability, and in litigation.

Chapter 14. Venture Capital

a. Procter ' Gamble	b. Valuation
c. Margin	d. Share

6. The term _____ has three unrelated technical definitions, and is also used in a variety of non-technical ways.

- In financial economics, it refers to any asset used to make money, as opposed to assets used for personal enjoyment or consumption. This is an important distinction because two people can disagree sharply about the value of personal assets, one person might think a sports car is more valuable than a pickup truck, another person might have the opposite taste. But if an asset is held for the purpose of making money, taste has nothing to do with it, only differences of opinion about how much money the asset will produce. With the further assumption that people agree on the probability distribution of future cash flows, it is possible to have an objective _____ pricing model. Even without the assumption of agreement, it is possible to set rational limits on _____ value.
- In governmental accounting, it is defined as any asset used in operations with an initial useful life extending beyond one reporting period. Generally, government managers have a 'stewardship' duty to maintain _____s under their control. See International Public Sector Accounting Standards for details.
- In US tax accounting, it is defined as any property other than a list of exceptions. The main exceptions are anything held for sale, and any real estate or depreciable property used in business. Almost everything you own and use for personal purposes, pleasure or investment is a _____. If something is a _____ for tax purposes, gains or losses on sale or disposition are capital gains or capital losses. For individuals, however, capital losses on property held for personal use are generally not deductible. See the IRS publication Tax Facts about Capital Gains and Losses for details.

A well-known financial accounting textbook advises that the term be avoided except in tax accounting because it is used in so many different senses, not all of them well-defined. For example it is often used as a synonym for fixed assets or for investments in securities.

A common non-technical usage occurs when people ask that employees or the environment or something else be treated as a _____.

a. Political risk	b. Settlement date
c. Solvency	d. Capital Asset

7. In finance, the _____ is used to determine a theoretically appropriate required rate of return of an asset, if that asset is to be added to an already well-diversified portfolio, given that asset's non-diversifiable risk. The model takes into account the asset's sensitivity to non-diversifiable risk (also known as systemic risk or market risk), often represented by the quantity beta (β) in the financial industry, as well as the expected return of the market and the expected return of a theoretical risk-free asset.

The model was introduced by Jack Treynor (1961, 1962), William Sharpe (1964), John Lintner (1965a,b) and Jan Mossin (1966) independently, building on the earlier work of Harry Markowitz on diversification and modern portfolio theory.

a. Random walk hypothesis	b. Capital Asset Pricing Model
c. Hull-White model	d. Cox-Ingersoll-Ross model

Chapter 14. Venture Capital

8. The _____ of 1974 (Pub.L. 93-406, 88 Stat. 829, enacted September 2, 1974) is an American federal statute that establishes minimum standards for pension plans in private industry and provides for extensive rules on the federal income tax effects of transactions associated with employee benefit plans.
   a. Expedited Funds Availability Act
   b. Articles of Partnership
   c. Express warranty
   d. Employee Retirement Income Security Act

9. _____, refers to consumption opportunity gained by an entity within a specified time frame, which is generally expressed in monetary terms. However, for households and individuals, '_____ is the sum of all the wages, salaries, profits, interests payments, rents and other forms of earnings received... in a given period of time.' For firms, _____ generally refers to net-profit: what remains of revenue after expenses have been subtracted.
   a. Accrual
   b. Annual report
   c. OIBDA
   d. Income

10. An _____ is a company whose main business is holding securities of other companies purely for investment purposes. The _____ invests money on behalf of its shareholders who in turn share in the profits and losses.
    a. AAB
    b. Unit investment trust
    c. Investment company
    d. A Random Walk Down Wall Street

11. A _____ is a fungible, negotiable instrument representing financial value. They are broadly categorized into debt securities (such as banknotes, bonds and debentures), and equity securities; e.g., common stocks. The company or other entity issuing the _____ is called the issuer.
    a. Book entry
    b. Tracking stock
    c. Securities lending
    d. Security

12. The U.S. _____ is an independent agency of the United States government which holds primary responsibility for enforcing the federal securities laws and regulating the securities industry, the nation's stock and options exchanges, and other electronic securities markets. The SEC was created by section 4 of the SEC of 1934 (now codified as 15 U.S.C. Â§ 78d and commonly referred to as the 1934 Act.)
    a. 4-4-5 Calendar
    b. Securities and Exchange Commission
    c. 7-Eleven
    d. 529 plan

13. A _____ or bank is a financial institution whose primary activity is to act as a payment agent for customers and to borrow and lend money.

The first modern bank was founded in Italy in Genoa in 1406, its name was Banco di San Giorgio (Bank of St. George.)

Many other financial activities were added over time.

   a. Banker
   b. 4-4-5 Calendar
   c. Black Sea Trade and Development Bank
   d. Bought deal

14. The _____ is the market for securities, where companies and governments can raise longterm funds. The _____ includes the stock market and the bond market. Financial regulators, such as the U.S. Securities and Exchange Commission, oversee the _____s in their designated countries to ensure that investors are protected against fraud.

a. Delta neutral
b. Spot rate
c. Forward market
d. Capital market

15. In economics, business, and accounting, a _____ is the value of money that has been used up to produce something, and hence is not available for use anymore. In business, the _____ may be one of acquisition, in which case the amount of money expended to acquire it is counted as _____. In this case, money is the input that is gone in order to acquire the thing.
   a. Sliding scale fees
   b. Fixed costs
   c. Marginal cost
   d. Cost

16. The _____ is an expected return that the provider of capital plans to earn on their investment.

Capital (money) used for funding a business should earn returns for the capital providers who risk their capital. For an investment to be worthwhile, the expected return on capital must be greater than the _____.

   a. 4-4-5 Calendar
   b. Capital intensity
   c. Weighted average cost of capital
   d. Cost of capital

17. _____ are organizations which pool large sums of money and invest those sums in companies. They include banks, insurance companies, retirement or pension funds, hedge funds and mutual funds. Their role in the economy is to act as highly specialized investors on behalf of others.
   a. AAB
   b. ABN Amro
   c. Institutional investors
   d. A Random Walk Down Wall Street

18. The phrase _____ according to the Organization for Economic Co-operation and Development, refers to 'creative work undertaken on a systematic basis in order to increase the stock of knowledge, including knowledge of (hu)man, culture and society, and the use of this stock of knowledge to devise new applications'.

New product design and development is more than often a crucial factor in the survival of a company. In an industry that is fast changing, firms must continually revise their design and range of products. This is necessary due to continuous technology change and development as well as other competitors and the changing preference of customers.

   a. 4-4-5 Calendar
   b. 529 plan
   c. 7-Eleven
   d. Research and development

19. _____ is a term used to describe the value of an entity's assets less the value of its liabilities. The term is commonly used in relation to collective investment schemes. It may also be used as a synonym for the book value of a firm.
   a. Retail broker
   b. Passive management
   c. Financial intermediary
   d. Net asset value

20. _____, is when a company issues common stock or shares to the public for the first time. They are often issued by smaller, younger companies seeking capital to expand, but can also be done by large privately-owned companies looking to become publicly traded.

In an _____ the issuer may obtain the assistance of an underwriting firm, which helps it determine what type of security to issue (common or preferred), best offering price and time to bring it to market.

   a. Asian Financial Crisis
   c. Interest

   b. Insolvency
   d. Initial public offering

21. A _____ or equity fund is a fund that invests in Equities more commonly known as stocks. Such funds are typically held either in stock or cash, as opposed to Bonds, notes, or other securities. This may be a mutual fund or exchange-traded fund.

   a. Mutual fund fees and expenses
   c. Closed-end fund

   b. Money market funds
   d. Stock fund

22. An _____ is a contract written by a seller that conveys to the buyer the right -- but not the obligation -- to buy (in the case of a call _____) or to sell (in the case of a put _____) a particular asset, such as a piece of property such as, among others, a futures contract. In return for granting the _____, the seller collects a payment (the premium) from the buyer.

For example, buying a call _____ provides the right to buy a specified quantity of a security at a set strike price at some time on or before expiration, while buying a put _____ provides the right to sell.

   a. Amortization
   c. AT'T Mobility LLC

   b. Annuity
   d. Option

23. A _____ is a type of business entity in which partners (owners) share with each other the profits or losses of the business undertaking in which all have invested. _____s are often favored over corporations for taxation purposes, as the _____ structure does not generally incur a tax on profits before it is distributed to the partners (i.e. there is no dividend tax levied.) However, depending on the _____ structure and the jurisdiction in which it operates, owners of a _____ may be exposed to greater personal liability than they would as shareholders of a corporation.

   a. Partnership
   c. Fiduciary

   b. Clayton Antitrust Act
   d. National Securities Markets Improvement Act of 1996

24. A _____ is a corporation in the United States that, for Federal income tax purposes, is taxed under 26 U.S.C. § 11 and Subchapter C (26 U.S.C. § 11 and Subchapter C (26 U.S.C. § 301 et seq.) of Chapter 1 of the Internal Revenue Code. Most major companies (and many smaller companies) are treated as _____ for Federal income tax purposes.

The income of a _____ is taxed, whereas the income of an S corporation (with a few exceptions) is not taxed under the Federal income tax laws. The income, or loss, is applied, Pro Rata, to each Shareholder and appears on their tax return as Schedule E income/(loss).

   a. 7-Eleven
   c. 529 plan

   b. 4-4-5 Calendar
   d. C corporation

Chapter 14. Venture Capital

25. The institution most often referenced by the word '_____' is a public or publicly traded _____, the shares of which are traded on a public stock exchange (e.g., the New York Stock Exchange or Nasdaq in the United States) where shares of stock of _____s are bought and sold by and to the general public. Most of the largest businesses in the world are publicly traded _____s. However, the majority of _____s are said to be closely held, privately held or close _____s, meaning that no ready market exists for the trading of shares.
    a. Protect
    b. Corporation
    c. Federal Home Loan Mortgage Corporation
    d. Depository Trust Company

26. _____ refers to the additional value of a commodity over the cost of commodities used to produce it from the previous stage of production. An example is the price of gasoline at the pump over the price of the oil in it. In national accounts used in macroeconomics, it refers to the contribution of the factors of production, i.e., land, labor, and capital goods, to raising the value of a product and corresponds to the incomes received by the owners of these factors.
    a. Deregulation
    b. Demand shock
    c. Supply shock
    d. Value added

27. _____ refers to the stock of skills and knowledge embodied in the ability to perform labor so as to produce economic value. Many early economic theories refer to it simply as labor, one of three factors of production, and consider it to be a fungible resource -- homogeneous and easily interchangeable. Other conceptions of labor dispense with these assumptions.
    a. Behavioral finance
    b. Human capital
    c. Market structure
    d. Mercantilism

28. In financial accounting, _____s are precautions for which the amount or probability of occurrence are not known. Typical examples are _____s for warranty costs and _____ for taxes the term reserve is used instead of term _____; such a use, however, is inconsistent with the terminology suggested by International Accounting Standards Board.
    a. Provision
    b. Momentum Accounting and Triple-Entry Bookkeeping
    c. Money measurement concept
    d. Petty cash

29. _____ or financing is to provide capital (funds), which means money for a project, a person, a business or any other private or public institutions.

    Those funds can be allocated for either short term or long term purposes. The health fund is a new way of _____ private healthcare centers.

    a. Synthetic CDO
    b. Product life cycle
    c. Proxy fight
    d. Funding

30. In the United States, a _____ is an offering of securities that are not registered with the Securities and Exchange Commission (SEC.) Such offerings exploit an exemption offered by the Securities Act of 1933 that comes with several restrictions, including a prohibition against general solicitation. This exemption allows companies to avoid quarterly reporting requirements and many of the legal liabilities associated with the Sarbanes-Oxley Act.
    a. 4-4-5 Calendar
    b. 7-Eleven
    c. 529 plan
    d. Private placement

Chapter 14. Venture Capital

31. A _____ is an exchange of promises between two or more parties to do an act which is enforceable in a court of law. It is where an unqualified offer meets a qualified acceptance and the parties reach Consensus ad Idem. The parties must have the necessary capacity to _____ and the _____ must not be either trifling, indeterminate, impossible or illegal.
    a. 7-Eleven
    b. 4-4-5 Calendar
    c. 529 plan
    d. Contract

32. An _____ is a call option on the common stock of a company, issued as a form of non-cash compensation. Restrictions on the option (such as vesting and limited transferability) attempt to align the holder's interest with those of the business' shareholders. If the company's stock rises, holders of options experience a direct financial benefit.
    a. Internal financing
    b. Underwriting contract
    c. Operating ratio
    d. Employee stock Option

33. An _____ is a corporation that makes a valid election to be taxed under Subchapter S of Chapter 1 of the Internal Revenue Code.

    In general, _____s do not pay any income taxes. Instead, the corporation's income or losses are divided among and passed through to its shareholders.

    a. 4-4-5 Calendar
    b. 529 plan
    c. 7-Eleven
    d. S corporation

34. _____ refers to the methods of practicing and using another person's business philosophy. The franchisor grants the independent operator the right to distribute its products, techniques, and trademarks for a percentage of gross monthly sales and a royalty fee. Various tangibles and intangibles such as national or international advertising, training, and other support services are commonly made available by the franchisor.
    a. Franchising
    b. 7-Eleven
    c. 4-4-5 Calendar
    d. 529 plan

35. The term _____ refers to three closely related concepts:

    - The _____ model is a mathematical model of the market for an equity, in which the equity's price is a stochastic process.
    - The _____ PDE is a partial differential equation which (in the model) must be satisfied by the price of a derivative on the equity.
    - The _____ formula is the result obtained by solving the _____ PDE for a European call option.

    Fischer Black and Myron Scholes first articulated the _____ formula in their 1973 paper, 'The Pricing of Options and Corporate Liabilities.' The foundation for their research relied on work developed by scholars such as Jack L. Treynor, Paul Samuelson, A. James Boness, Sheen T. Kassouf, and Edward O. Thorp. The fundamental insight of _____ is that the option is implicitly priced if the stock is traded.

    Robert C. Merton was the first to publish a paper expanding the mathematical understanding of the options pricing model and coined the term '_____' options pricing model.

Chapter 14. Venture Capital

a. Perpetuity
c. Black-Scholes
b. Modified Internal Rate of Return
d. Stochastic volatility

36. An _____ or angel is an affluent individual who provides capital for a business start-up, usually in exchange for convertible debt or ownership equity. A small but increasing number of _____s organize themselves into angel groups or angel networks to share research and pool their investment capital.

Angels typically invest their own funds, unlike venture capitalists, who manage the pooled money of others in a professionally-managed fund.

a. AAB
c. ABN Amro
b. A Random Walk Down Wall Street
d. Angel investor

37. The _____ is the guaranteed payoff at which a person is 'indifferent' between accepting the guaranteed payoff and a higher but uncertain payoff. (It is the amount of the higher payout minus the risk premium).

a. 7-Eleven
c. 4-4-5 Calendar
b. 529 plan
d. Certainty equivalent

38. _____ is the provision of resources (such as granting a loan) by one party to another party where that second party does not reimburse the first party immediately, thereby generating a debt, and instead arranges either to repay or return those resources (or material(s) of equal value) at a later date. The first party is called a creditor, also known as a lender, while the second party is called a debtor, also known as a borrower.

Movements of financial capital are normally dependent on either _____ or equity transfers.

a. Comparable
c. Warrant
b. Clearing house
d. Credit

39. _____ is a financial transaction whereby a business sells its accounts receivable (i.e., invoices) at a discount. _____ differs from a bank loan in three main ways. First, the emphasis is on the value of the receivables (essentially a financial asset), not the firm's credit worthiness.

a. Credit card balance transfer
c. Financial Literacy Month
b. Debt-for-equity swap
d. Factoring

40. _____ is a process by which a firm can obtain the use of a certain fixed assets for which it must pay a series of contractual, periodic, tax deductable payments. The lessee is the receiver of the services or the assets under the lease contract and the lessor is the owner of the assets. The relationship between the tenant and the landlord is called a tenancy, and can be for a fixed or an indefinite period of time (called the term of the lease).

a. Quiet period
c. Foreign Corrupt Practices Act
b. Royalties
d. Leasing

41. _____ right are usage-based payments made by one party to another (the 'licensor') for ongoing use of an asset, sometimes an intellectual property (IP) right..

_____ can be determined as a percentage of gross or net sales derived from use of the asset or a fixed price per unit sold. but there are also other modes and metrics of compensation.

a. Due diligence
b. Celler-Kefauver Act
c. Financial Institutions Reform Recovery and Enforcement Act
d. Royalties

42. _____ exists when one firm provides goods or services to a customer with an agreement to bill them later, or receive a shipment or service from a supplier under an agreement to pay them later. It can be viewed as an essential element of capitalization in an operating business because it can reduce the required capital investment to operate the business if it is managed properly. _____ is the largest use of capital for a majority of business to business (B2B) sellers in the United States and is a critical source of capital for a majority of all businesses.
   a. Going concern
   b. 4-4-5 Calendar
   c. 529 plan
   d. Trade credit

43. _____ can be regarded as an outcome of mental processes (cognitive process) leading to the selection of a course of action among several alternatives. Every _____ process produces a final choice. The output can be an action or an opinion of choice.
   a. Decision making
   b. 4-4-5 Calendar
   c. 7-Eleven
   d. 529 plan

44. _____ are legal property rights over creations of the mind, both artistic and commercial, and the corresponding fields of law. Under _____ law, owners are granted certain exclusive rights to a variety of intangible assets, such as musical, literary, and artistic works; ideas, discoveries and inventions; and words, phrases, symbols, and designs. Common types of _____ include copyrights, trademarks, patents, industrial design rights and trade secrets.
   a. ABN Amro
   b. A Random Walk Down Wall Street
   c. Intellectual property
   d. AAB

45. A sole _____, or simply _____ is a type of business entity which legally has no separate existence from its owner. Hence, the limitations of liability enjoyed by a corporation and limited liability partnerships do not apply to sole proprietors. All debts of the business are debts of the owner.
   a. Product life cycle
   b. Proprietorship
   c. Free cash flow
   d. Just-in-time

46. _____ is an organization's process of defining its strategy and making decisions on allocating its resources to pursue this strategy, including its capital and people. Various business analysis techniques can be used in _____, including SWOT analysis (Strengths, Weaknesses, Opportunities, and Threats) and PEST analysis (Political, Economic, Social, and Technological analysis) or STEER analysis involving Socio-cultural, Technological, Economic, Ecological, and Regulatory factors and EPISTEL (Environment, Political, Informatic, Social, Technological, Economic and Legal)

_____ is the formal consideration of an organization's future course. All _____ deals with at least one of three key questions:

1. 'What do we do?'
2. 'For whom do we do it?'
3. 'How do we excel?'

In business _____, the third question is better phrased 'How can we beat or avoid competition?'. (Bradford and Duncan, page 1.)

Chapter 14. Venture Capital

a. 529 plan
b. 7-Eleven
c. 4-4-5 Calendar
d. Strategic planning

47. A _____ is a decision support tool that uses a tree-like graph or model of decisions and their possible consequences, including chance event outcomes, resource costs, and utility. _____s are commonly used in operations research, specifically in decision analysis, to help identify a strategy most likely to reach a goal. Another use of _____s is as a descriptive means for calculating conditional probabilities.

a. 4-4-5 Calendar
b. Decision tree
c. 529 plan
d. 7-Eleven

48. _____ is a process of analyzing possible future events by considering alternative possible outcomes (scenarios.) The analysis is designed to allow improved decision-making by allowing consideration of outcomes and their implications.

For example, in economics and finance, a financial institution might attempt to forecast several possible scenarios for the economy (e.g. rapid growth, moderate growth, slow growth) and it might also attempt to forecast financial market returns (for bonds, stocks and cash) in each of those scenarios.

a. 4-4-5 Calendar
b. 529 plan
c. Detection Risk
d. Scenario analysis

49. A _____ is a form of partnership similar to a general partnership, except that in addition to one or more general partners (GPs), there are one or more limited partners (_____s). It is a partnership in which only one partner is required to be a general partner.

The GPs are, in all major respects, in the same legal position as partners in a conventional firm, i.e. they have management control, share the right to use partnership property, share the profits of the firm in predefined proportions, and have joint and several liability for the debts of the partnership.

a. Limited liability company
b. Fund of funds
c. Leverage
d. Limited partnership

50. A _____, in its most general sense, is a solemn promise to engage in or refrain from a specified action.

More specifically, a _____, in contrast to a contract, is a one-way agreement whereby the _____er is the only party bound by the promise. A _____ may have conditions and prerequisites that qualify the undertaking, including the actions of second or third parties, but there is no inherent agreement by such other parties to fulfill those requirements.

a. Partnership
b. Clayton Antitrust Act
c. Federal Trade Commission Act
d. Covenant

51. In finance and economics, _____ or divestiture is the reduction of some kind of asset for either financial goals or ethical objectives. A _____ is the opposite of an investment.

Often the term is used as a means to grow financially in which a company sells off a business unit in order to focus their resources on a market it judges to be more profitable, or promising.

   a. Late trading
   b. Divestment
   c. Portfolio investment
   d. Certificate in Investment Performance Measurement

52. _____ is the balance of the amounts of cash being received and paid by a business during a defined period of time, sometimes tied to a specific project. Measurement of _____ can be used

- to evaluate the state or performance of a business or project.
- to determine problems with liquidity. Being profitable does not necessarily mean being liquid. A company can fail because of a shortage of cash, even while profitable.
- to generate project rate of returns. The time of _____s into and out of projects are used as inputs to financial models such as internal rate of return, and net present value.
- to examine income or growth of a business when it is believed that accrual accounting concepts do not represent economic realities. Alternately, _____ can be used to 'validate' the net income generated by accrual accounting.

_____ as a generic term may be used differently depending on context, and certain _____ definitions may be adapted by analysts and users for their own uses. Common terms include operating _____ and free _____.

_____s can be classified into:

1. Operational _____s: Cash received or expended as a result of the company's core business activities.
2. Investment _____s: Cash received or expended through capital expenditure, investments or acquisitions.
3. Financing _____s: Cash received or expended as a result of financial activities, such as interests and dividends.

All three together - the net _____ - are necessary to reconcile the beginning cash balance to the ending cash balance. Loan draw downs or equity injections, that is just shifting of capital but no expenditure as such, are not considered in the net _____.

   a. Real option
   b. Cash flow
   c. Corporate finance
   d. Shareholder value

53. _____ is a term in Corporate Finance used to indicate a condition when promises to creditors of a company are broken or honored with difficulty. Sometimes _____ can lead to bankruptcy. _____ is usually associated with some costs to the company and these are known as Costs of _____.

   a. Commercial paper
   b. Cashflow matching
   c. Capital structure
   d. Financial distress

Chapter 14. Venture Capital

54. _____ is a legally declared inability or impairment of ability of an individual or organization to pay their creditors. Creditors may file a _____ petition against a debtor ('involuntary _____') in an effort to recoup a portion of what they are owed or initiate a restructuring. In the majority of cases, however, _____ is initiated by the debtor (a 'voluntary _____' that is filed by the bankrupt individual or organization.)

  a. Debt settlement
  b. 529 plan
  c. 4-4-5 Calendar
  d. Bankruptcy

55. _____ is the price at which an asset would trade in a competitive Walrasian auction setting. _____ is often used interchangeably with open _____, fair value or fair _____, although these terms have distinct definitions in different standards, and may differ in some circumstances.

International Valuation Standards defines _____ as 'the estimated amount for which a property should exchange on the date of valuation between a willing buyer and a willing seller in an arm'e;s-length transaction after proper marketing wherein the parties had each acted knowledgeably, prudently, and without compulsion.'

_____ is a concept distinct from market price, which is 'e;the price at which one can transact'e;, while _____ is 'e;the true underlying value'e; according to theoretical standards.

  a. T-Model
  b. Wrap account
  c. Debt restructuring
  d. Market value

Chapter 15. Harvesting

1. A '_____' is a 'Charge' that is paid to obtain the right to delay a payment. Essentially, the payer purchases the right to make a given payment in the future instead of in the Present. The '_____', or 'Charge' that must be paid to delay the payment, is simply the difference between what the payment amount would be if it were paid in the present and what the payment amount would be paid if it were paid in the future.

   a. Risk aversion
   b. Risk modeling
   c. Value at risk
   d. Discount

2. The _____ is an interest rate a central bank charges depository institutions that borrow reserves from it.

   The term _____ has two meanings:

   - the same as interest rate; the term 'discount' does not refer to the meaning of the word, but to the purpose of using the quantity, such as computations of present value, e.g. net present value / discounted cash flow

   - the annual effective _____, which is the annual interest divided by the capital including that interest; this rate is lower than the interest rate; it corresponds to using the value after a year as the nominal value, and seeing the initial value as the nominal value minus a discount; it is used for Treasury Bills and similar financial instruments

   The annual effective _____ is the annual interest divided by the capital including that interest, which is the interest rate divided by 100% plus the interest rate. It is the annual discount factor to be applied to the future cash flow, to find the discount, subtracted from a future value to find the value one year earlier.

   For example, suppose there is a government bond that sells for $95 and pays $100 in a year's time.

   a. Fisher equation
   b. Stochastic volatility
   c. Black-Scholes
   d. Discount Rate

3. _____ is a type of private equity capital typically provided to early-stage, high-potential, growth companies in the interest of generating a return through an eventual realization event such as an IPO or trade sale of the company. _____ investments are generally made as cash in exchange for shares in the invested company. It is typical for _____ investors to identify and back companies in high technology industries such as biotechnology and ICT.

   a. Tail risk
   b. Venture Capital
   c. Probability distribution
   d. Treasury Inflation-Protected Securities

4. The term _____ refers to three closely related concepts:

   - The _____ model is a mathematical model of the market for an equity, in which the equity's price is a stochastic process.
   - The _____ PDE is a partial differential equation which (in the model) must be satisfied by the price of a derivative on the equity.
   - The _____ formula is the result obtained by solving the _____ PDE for a European call option.

Chapter 15. Harvesting

Fischer Black and Myron Scholes first articulated the _____ formula in their 1973 paper, 'The Pricing of Options and Corporate Liabilities.' The foundation for their research relied on work developed by scholars such as Jack L. Treynor, Paul Samuelson, A. James Boness, Sheen T. Kassouf, and Edward O. Thorp. The fundamental insight of _____ is that the option is implicitly priced if the stock is traded.

Robert C. Merton was the first to publish a paper expanding the mathematical understanding of the options pricing model and coined the term '_____' options pricing model.

- a. Perpetuity
- c. Stochastic volatility
- b. Black-Scholes
- d. Modified Internal Rate of Return

5. A _____ is a corporation in the United States that, for Federal income tax purposes, is taxed under 26 U.S.C. § 11 and Subchapter C (26 U.S.C. § 11 and Subchapter C (26 U.S.C. § 301 et seq.) of Chapter 1 of the Internal Revenue Code. Most major companies (and many smaller companies) are treated as _____ for Federal income tax purposes.

The income of a _____ is taxed, whereas the income of an S corporation (with a few exceptions) is not taxed under the Federal income tax laws. The income, or loss, is applied, Pro Rata, to each Shareholder and appears on their tax return as Schedule E income/(loss).

- a. C corporation
- c. 4-4-5 Calendar
- b. 7-Eleven
- d. 529 plan

6. An _____ is a contract written by a seller that conveys to the buyer the right -- but not the obligation -- to buy (in the case of a call _____) or to sell (in the case of a put _____) a particular asset, such as a piece of property such as, among others, a futures contract. In return for granting the _____, the seller collects a payment (the premium) from the buyer.

For example, buying a call _____ provides the right to buy a specified quantity of a security at a set strike price at some time on or before expiration, while buying a put _____ provides the right to sell.

- a. Annuity
- c. AT'T Mobility LLC
- b. Amortization
- d. Option

7. An _____ is a corporation that makes a valid election to be taxed under Subchapter S of Chapter 1 of the Internal Revenue Code.

In general, _____s do not pay any income taxes. Instead, the corporation's income or losses are divided among and passed through to its shareholders.

- a. 7-Eleven
- c. 529 plan
- b. S corporation
- d. 4-4-5 Calendar

8. The institution most often referenced by the word '_____' is a public or publicly traded _____, the shares of which are traded on a public stock exchange (e.g., the New York Stock Exchange or Nasdaq in the United States) where shares of stock of _____s are bought and sold by and to the general public. Most of the largest businesses in the world are publicly traded _____s. However, the majority of _____s are said to be closely held, privately held or close _____s, meaning that no ready market exists for the trading of shares.

   a. Protect
   b. Depository Trust Company
   c. Federal Home Loan Mortgage Corporation
   d. Corporation

9. In economics, business, and accounting, a _____ is the value of money that has been used up to produce something, and hence is not available for use anymore. In business, the _____ may be one of acquisition, in which case the amount of money expended to acquire it is counted as _____. In this case, money is the input that is gone in order to acquire the thing.

   a. Sliding scale fees
   b. Cost
   c. Marginal cost
   d. Fixed costs

10. The _____ is an expected return that the provider of capital plans to earn on their investment.

Capital (money) used for funding a business should earn returns for the capital providers who risk their capital. For an investment to be worthwhile, the expected return on capital must be greater than the _____.

   a. Weighted average cost of capital
   b. Capital intensity
   c. 4-4-5 Calendar
   d. Cost of capital

11. _____, is when a company issues common stock or shares to the public for the first time. They are often issued by smaller, younger companies seeking capital to expand, but can also be done by large privately-owned companies looking to become publicly traded.

In an _____ the issuer may obtain the assistance of an underwriting firm, which helps it determine what type of security to issue (common or preferred), best offering price and time to bring it to market.

   a. Insolvency
   b. Initial public offering
   c. Asian Financial Crisis
   d. Interest

12. The _____ of 1974 (Pub.L. 93-406, 88 Stat. 829, enacted September 2, 1974) is an American federal statute that establishes minimum standards for pension plans in private industry and provides for extensive rules on the federal income tax effects of transactions associated with employee benefit plans.

   a. Express warranty
   b. Expedited Funds Availability Act
   c. Articles of Partnership
   d. Employee Retirement Income Security Act

13. _____, refers to consumption opportunity gained by an entity within a specified time frame, which is generally expressed in monetary terms. However, for households and individuals, '_____ is the sum of all the wages, salaries, profits, interests payments, rents and other forms of earnings received... in a given period of time.' For firms, _____ generally refers to net-profit: what remains of revenue after expenses have been subtracted.

   a. Income
   b. Accrual
   c. OIBDA
   d. Annual report

Chapter 15. Harvesting

14. A _____ is a fungible, negotiable instrument representing financial value. They are broadly categorized into debt securities (such as banknotes, bonds and debentures), and equity securities; e.g., common stocks. The company or other entity issuing the _____ is called the issuer.
 a. Security
 b. Book entry
 c. Tracking stock
 d. Securities lending

15. The _____ of a stock is a measure of the price paid for a share relative to the annual income or profit earned by the firm per share. It is a financial ratio used for valuation: a higher _____ means that investors are paying more for each unit of income, so the stock is more expensive compared to one with lower _____.

The _____ has units of years, which can be interpreted as 'number of years of earnings to pay back purchase price'.

 a. Return of capital
 b. Sustainable growth rate
 c. Quick ratio
 d. P/E ratio

16. _____ is a financial metric which represents operating liquidity available to a business. Along with fixed assets such as plant and equipment, _____ is considered a part of operating capital. It is calculated as current assets minus current liabilities.
 a. Working capital management
 b. 529 plan
 c. 4-4-5 Calendar
 d. Working capital

17. An _____ is a company whose main business is holding securities of other companies purely for investment purposes. The _____ invests money on behalf of its shareholders who in turn share in the profits and losses.
 a. A Random Walk Down Wall Street
 b. AAB
 c. Unit investment trust
 d. Investment Company

18. _____ is that which is owed; usually referencing assets owed, but the term can cover other obligations. In the case of assets, _____ is a means of using future purchasing power in the present before a summation has been earned. Some companies and corporations use _____ as a part of their overall corporate finance strategy.
 a. Partial Payment
 b. Credit cycle
 c. Debt
 d. Cross-collateralization

19. In the theory of capital structure, _____ is the phrase used to describe funds that firms obtain from outside of the firm. It is contrasted to internal financing which consists mainly of profits retained by the firm for investment. There are many kinds of _____.
 a. Ownership equity
 b. Asset-backed commercial paper
 c. External financing
 d. Adjustment

20. _____ or financing is to provide capital (funds), which means money for a project, a person, a business or any other private or public institutions.

Those funds can be allocated for either short term or long term purposes. The health fund is a new way of _____ private healthcare centers.

Chapter 15. Harvesting

a. Product life cycle
b. Synthetic CDO
c. Funding
d. Proxy fight

21. In the _____ contract the underwriter guarantees the sale of the issued stock at the agreed-upon price. For the issuer, it is the safest but the most expensive type of the contracts, since the underwriter takes the risk of sale.

In the best efforts contract the underwriter agrees to sell as many shares as possible at the agreed-upon price.

a. Special purpose entity
b. Firm commitment
c. Participating preferred stock
d. Rights issue

22. In finance, a _____ is a security that entitles the holder to buy stock of the company that issued it at a specified price, which is usually higher than the stock price at time of issue.

_____s are frequently attached to bonds or preferred stock as a sweetener, allowing the issuer to pay lower interest rates or dividends. They can be used to enhance the yield of the bond, and make them more attractive to potential buyers.

a. Clearing
b. Clearing house
c. Credit
d. Warrant

23. A _____ is a decision support tool that uses a tree-like graph or model of decisions and their possible consequences, including chance event outcomes, resource costs, and utility. _____s are commonly used in operations research, specifically in decision analysis, to help identify a strategy most likely to reach a goal. Another use of _____s is as a descriptive means for calculating conditional probabilities.

a. 7-Eleven
b. 529 plan
c. 4-4-5 Calendar
d. Decision tree

24. The U.S. _____ is an independent agency of the United States government which holds primary responsibility for enforcing the federal securities laws and regulating the securities industry, the nation's stock and options exchanges, and other electronic securities markets. The SEC was created by section 4 of the SEC of 1934 (now codified as 15 U.S.C. Â§ 78d and commonly referred to as the 1934 Act.)

a. 4-4-5 Calendar
b. 529 plan
c. 7-Eleven
d. Securities and Exchange Commission

25. An _____ or angel is an affluent individual who provides capital for a business start-up, usually in exchange for convertible debt or ownership equity. A small but increasing number of _____s organize themselves into angel groups or angel networks to share research and pool their investment capital.

Angels typically invest their own funds, unlike venture capitalists, who manage the pooled money of others in a professionally-managed fund.

a. ABN Amro
b. AAB
c. Angel investor
d. A Random Walk Down Wall Street

Chapter 15. Harvesting

26. The phrase _____ refers to the aspect of corporate strategy, corporate finance and management dealing with the buying, selling and combining of different companies that can aid, finance, or help a growing company in a given industry grow rapidly without having to create another business entity.

An acquisition, also known as a takeover, is the buying of one company (the 'target') by another. An acquisition may be friendly or hostile.

a. 529 plan
c. 4-4-5 Calendar
b. Mergers and acquisitions
d. 7-Eleven

27. _____ can be regarded as an outcome of mental processes (cognitive process) leading to the selection of a course of action among several alternatives. Every _____ process produces a final choice. The output can be an action or an opinion of choice.

a. 529 plan
c. 4-4-5 Calendar
b. Decision making
d. 7-Eleven

28. _____ refers to a business or organization attempting to acquire goods or services to accomplish the goals of the enterprise. Though there are several organizations that attempt to set standards in the _____ process, processes can vary greatly between organizations. Typically the word '_____' is not used interchangeably with the word 'procurement', since procurement typically includes Expediting, Supplier Quality, and Traffic and Logistics (T'L) in addition to _____.

a. 529 plan
c. 7-Eleven
b. 4-4-5 Calendar
d. Purchasing

29. In business and finance, a _____ (also referred to as equity _____) of stock means a _____ of ownership in a corporation (company.) In the plural, stocks is often used as a synonym for _____s especially in the United States, but it is less commonly used that way outside of North America.

In the United Kingdom, South Africa, and Australia, stock can also refer to completely different financial instruments such as government bonds or, less commonly, to all kinds of marketable securities.

a. Bucket shop
c. Margin
b. Procter ' Gamble
d. Share

30. _____ is an organization's process of defining its strategy and making decisions on allocating its resources to pursue this strategy, including its capital and people. Various business analysis techniques can be used in _____, including SWOT analysis (Strengths, Weaknesses, Opportunities, and Threats) and PEST analysis (Political, Economic, Social, and Technological analysis) or STEER analysis involving Socio-cultural, Technological, Economic, Ecological, and Regulatory factors and EPISTEL (Environment, Political, Informatic, Social, Technological, Economic and Legal)

_____ is the formal consideration of an organization's future course. All _____ deals with at least one of three key questions:

1. 'What do we do?'
2. 'For whom do we do it?'
3. 'How do we excel?'

In business _____, the third question is better phrased 'How can we beat or avoid competition?'. (Bradford and Duncan, page 1.)

a. 7-Eleven
b. 529 plan
c. 4-4-5 Calendar
d. Strategic planning

31. _____, in bookkeeping, refers to assets, liabilities, income, and expenses recorded on individual pages of the so called book of final entry or ledger. Changes in _____ value are made by chronologically posting debit (DR) and credit (CR) entries to its page. Examples of _____s are cash, _____s receivable, mortgages, loans, land and buildings, common stock, sales, services provided, wages, and payroll overhead.

a. Option
b. Account
c. Accretion
d. Alpha

32. _____ is one of a series of accounting transactions dealing with the billing of customers who owe money to a person, company or organization for goods and services that have been provided to the customer. In most business entities this is typically done by generating an invoice and mailing or electronically delivering it to the customer, who in turn must pay it within an established timeframe called credit or payment terms.

An example of a common payment term is Net 30, meaning payment is due in the amount of the invoice 30 days from the date of invoice.

a. Income
b. Accounts receivable
c. Accounting methods
d. Impaired asset

33. In business and accounting, _____s are everything of value that is owned by a person or company. The balance sheet of a firm records the monetary value of the _____s owned by the firm. The two major _____ classes are tangible _____s and intangible _____s.

a. Income
b. Accounts payable
c. EBITDA
d. Asset

34. In finance, _____ is the process of estimating the potential market value of a financial asset or liability. they can be done on assets (for example, investments in marketable securities such as stocks, options, business enterprises, or intangible assets such as patents and trademarks) or on liabilities (e.g., Bonds issued by a company.) _____s are required in many contexts including investment analysis, capital budgeting, merger and acquisition transactions, financial reporting, taxable events to determine the proper tax liability, and in litigation.

a. Share
b. Procter ' Gamble
c. Valuation
d. Margin

Chapter 15. Harvesting

35. The term _____ has three unrelated technical definitions, and is also used in a variety of non-technical ways.

- In financial economics, it refers to any asset used to make money, as opposed to assets used for personal enjoyment or consumption. This is an important distinction because two people can disagree sharply about the value of personal assets, one person might think a sports car is more valuable than a pickup truck, another person might have the opposite taste. But if an asset is held for the purpose of making money, taste has nothing to do with it, only differences of opinion about how much money the asset will produce. With the further assumption that people agree on the probability distribution of future cash flows, it is possible to have an objective _____ pricing model. Even without the assumption of agreement, it is possible to set rational limits on _____ value.
- In governmental accounting, it is defined as any asset used in operations with an initial useful life extending beyond one reporting period. Generally, government managers have a 'stewardship' duty to maintain _____s under their control. See International Public Sector Accounting Standards for details.
- In US tax accounting, it is defined as any property other than a list of exceptions. The main exceptions are anything held for sale, and any real estate or depreciable property used in business. Almost everything you own and use for personal purposes, pleasure or investment is a _____. If something is a _____ for tax purposes, gains or losses on sale or disposition are capital gains or capital losses. For individuals, however, capital losses on property held for personal use are generally not deductible. See the IRS publication Tax Facts about Capital Gains and Losses for details.

A well-known financial accounting textbook advises that the term be avoided except in tax accounting because it is used in so many different senses, not all of them well-defined. For example it is often used as a synonym for fixed assets or for investments in securities.

A common non-technical usage occurs when people ask that employees or the environment or something else be treated as a _____.

a. Solvency
b. Settlement date
c. Capital Asset
d. Political risk

36. In finance, the _____ is used to determine a theoretically appropriate required rate of return of an asset, if that asset is to be added to an already well-diversified portfolio, given that asset's non-diversifiable risk. The model takes into account the asset's sensitivity to non-diversifiable risk (also known as systemic risk or market risk), often represented by the quantity beta (β) in the financial industry, as well as the expected return of the market and the expected return of a theoretical risk-free asset.

The model was introduced by Jack Treynor (1961, 1962), William Sharpe (1964), John Lintner (1965a,b) and Jan Mossin (1966) independently, building on the earlier work of Harry Markowitz on diversification and modern portfolio theory.

a. Cox-Ingersoll-Ross model
b. Hull-White model
c. Random walk hypothesis
d. Capital Asset Pricing Model

37. A _____ is a profit that results from investments into a capital asset, such as stocks, bonds or real estate, which exceeds the purchase price. It is the difference between a higher selling price and a lower purchase price, resulting in a financial gain for the seller. Conversely, a capital loss arises if the proceeds from the sale of a capital asset are less than the purchase price.

Chapter 15. Harvesting

a. Capital gains tax
b. Payroll tax
c. Tax brackets
d. Capital gain

38. _____ are costs incurred on the purchase of land, buildings, construction and equipment to be used in the production of goods or the rendering of services. In other words, the total cost needed to bring a project to a commercially operable status. However, _____ are not limited to the initial construction of a factory or other business.
   a. Capital outflow
   b. Defined contribution plan
   c. Trade-off
   d. Capital costs

39. A _____ is a pool of assets forming an independent legal entity that are bought with the contributions to a pension plan for the exclusive purpose of financing pension plan benefits.

_____s are important shareholders of listed and private companies. They are especially important to the stock market where large institutional investors like the Ontario Teachers' Pension Plan dominate.

   a. Leverage
   b. Pension fund
   c. Leveraged buyout
   d. Limited liability company

40. In the United States, a _____ is an offering of securities that are not registered with the Securities and Exchange Commission (SEC.) Such offerings exploit an exemption offered by the Securities Act of 1933 that comes with several restrictions, including a prohibition against general solicitation. This exemption allows companies to avoid quarterly reporting requirements and many of the legal liabilities associated with the Sarbanes-Oxley Act.
   a. 529 plan
   b. 4-4-5 Calendar
   c. 7-Eleven
   d. Private placement

41. In financial accounting, _____s are precautions for which the amount or probability of occurrence are not known. Typical examples are _____s for warranty costs and _____ for taxes the term reserve is used instead of term _____; such a use, however, is inconsistent with the terminology suggested by International Accounting Standards Board.
   a. Petty cash
   b. Momentum Accounting and Triple-Entry Bookkeeping
   c. Money measurement concept
   d. Provision

42. The _____ is the market for securities, where companies and governments can raise longterm funds. The _____ includes the stock market and the bond market. Financial regulators, such as the U.S. Securities and Exchange Commission, oversee the _____s in their designated countries to ensure that investors are protected against fraud.
   a. Forward market
   b. Spot rate
   c. Delta neutral
   d. Capital market

43. _____ is the price at which an asset would trade in a competitive Walrasian auction setting. _____ is often used interchangeably with open _____, fair value or fair _____, although these terms have distinct definitions in different standards, and may differ in some circumstances.

International Valuation Standards defines _____ as 'the estimated amount for which a property should exchange on the date of valuation between a willing buyer and a willing seller in an arm'e;s-length transaction after proper marketing wherein the parties had each acted knowledgeably, prudently, and without compulsion.'

Chapter 15. Harvesting

_____ is a concept distinct from market price, which is 'e;the price at which one can transact'e;, while _____ is 'e;the true underlying value'e; according to theoretical standards.

a. Wrap account
b. T-Model
c. Debt restructuring
d. Market value

44. _____ is typically a higher ranking stock than voting shares, and its terms are negotiated between the corporation and the investor.

_____ usually carry no voting rights, but may carry superior priority over common stock in the payment of dividends and upon liquidation. _____ may carry a dividend that is paid out prior to any dividends to common stock holders.

a. Second lien loan
b. Follow-on offering
c. Trade-off theory
d. Preferred stock

45. _____ is the acquisition of goods and/or services at the best possible total cost of ownership, in the right quantity and quality, at the right time, in the right place and from the right source for the direct benefit or use of corporations or individuals, generally via a contract. Simple _____ may involve nothing more than repeat purchasing. Complex _____ could involve finding long term partners - or even 'co-destiny' suppliers that might fundamentally commit one organization to another.

a. Pac-Man defense
b. Procurement
c. Market capitalization
d. Synthetic CDO

46. _____ according to Onuoha (2007) is the practice of starting new organizations or revitalizing mature organizations, particularly new businesses generally in response to identified opportunities. _____ is often a difficult undertaking, as a vast majority of new businesses fail. Entrepreneurial activities are substantially different depending on the type of organization that is being started.

a. Entrepreneurship
b. ABN Amro
c. A Random Walk Down Wall Street
d. AAB

47. In economics and contract theory, _____ deals with the study of decisions in transactions where one party has more or better information than the other. This creates an imbalance of power in transactions which can sometimes cause the transactions to go awry. Examples of this problem are adverse selection and moral hazard.

a. A Random Walk Down Wall Street
b. ABN Amro
c. AAB
d. Information asymmetry

48. The _____ or Venture Capital Method is a valuation method often used by venture capitalists and private equity professionals that combines elements of both a multiples-based valuation and a traditional discounted cash flow (DCF.) The method is particularly useful in valuing high-growth companies. Many practitioners feel that the method is better than a straight multiples method for valuing high-growth companies because high-growth companies do not have significant current financial results.

a. First Chicago method
b. Consumer basket
c. Sinking fund
d. Risk-return spectrum

Chapter 15. Harvesting

49. In corporate finance, _____ analysis applies put option and call option valuation techniques to capital budgeting decisions. A _____ itself, is the right--but not the obligation--to undertake some business decision; typically the option to make, or abandon, a capital investment. For example, the opportunity to invest in the expansion of a firm's factory, or alternatively to sell the factory, is a _____.
   a. Capital budgeting
   b. Book building
   c. Real Option
   d. Cash flow

50. _____ is the balance of the amounts of cash being received and paid by a business during a defined period of time, sometimes tied to a specific project. Measurement of _____ can be used

   - to evaluate the state or performance of a business or project.
   - to determine problems with liquidity. Being profitable does not necessarily mean being liquid. A company can fail because of a shortage of cash, even while profitable.
   - to generate project rate of returns. The time of _____s into and out of projects are used as inputs to financial models such as internal rate of return, and net present value.
   - to examine income or growth of a business when it is believed that accrual accounting concepts do not represent economic realities. Alternately, _____ can be used to 'validate' the net income generated by accrual accounting.

   _____ as a generic term may be used differently depending on context, and certain _____ definitions may be adapted by analysts and users for their own uses. Common terms include operating _____ and free _____.

   _____s can be classified into:

   1. Operational _____s: Cash received or expended as a result of the company's core business activities.
   2. Investment _____s: Cash received or expended through capital expenditure, investments or acquisitions.
   3. Financing _____s: Cash received or expended as a result of financial activities, such as interests and dividends.

   All three together - the net _____ - are necessary to reconcile the beginning cash balance to the ending cash balance. Loan draw downs or equity injections, that is just shifting of capital but no expenditure as such, are not considered in the net _____.

   a. Shareholder value
   b. Corporate finance
   c. Real option
   d. Cash flow

51. The _____ is the guaranteed payoff at which a person is 'indifferent' between accepting the guaranteed payoff and a higher but uncertain payoff. (It is the amount of the higher payout minus the risk premium).
   a. 7-Eleven
   b. 529 plan
   c. 4-4-5 Calendar
   d. Certainty equivalent

52. _____ or economic opportunity loss is the value of the next best alternative foregone as the result of making a decision. _____ analysis is an important part of a company's decision-making processes but is not treated as an actual cost in any financial statement. The next best thing that a person can engage in is referred to as the _____ of doing the best thing and ignoring the next best thing to be done.

Chapter 15. Harvesting　　127

　　a. ABN Amro　　　　　　　　　　　　　b. Opportunity cost
　　c. A Random Walk Down Wall Street　　d. AAB

53. _____ refers to the stock of skills and knowledge embodied in the ability to perform labor so as to produce economic value. Many early economic theories refer to it simply as labor, one of three factors of production, and consider it to be a fungible resource -- homogeneous and easily interchangeable. Other conceptions of labor dispense with these assumptions.
　　a. Market structure　　　　　　　　　b. Human capital
　　c. Behavioral finance　　　　　　　　d. Mercantilism

54. A _____ or bank is a financial institution whose primary activity is to act as a payment agent for customers and to borrow and lend money.

The first modern bank was founded in Italy in Genoa in 1406, its name was Banco di San Giorgio (Bank of St. George.)

Many other financial activities were added over time.

　　a. Black Sea Trade and Development Bank　　b. Banker
　　c. 4-4-5 Calendar　　　　　　　　　　　　　　d. Bought deal

55. _____ is a legally declared inability or impairment of ability of an individual or organization to pay their creditors. Creditors may file a _____ petition against a debtor ('involuntary _____') in an effort to recoup a portion of what they are owed or initiate a restructuring. In the majority of cases, however, _____ is initiated by the debtor (a 'voluntary _____' that is filed by the bankrupt individual or organization.)
　　a. Bankruptcy　　　　　　　　　　　　b. 529 plan
　　c. Debt settlement　　　　　　　　　　d. 4-4-5 Calendar

56. _____ is the increase in the amount of the goods and services produced by an economy over time. It is conventionally measured as the percent rate of increase in real gross domestic product, or real GDP. Growth is usually calculated in real terms, i.e. inflation-adjusted terms, in order to net out the effect of inflation on the price of the goods and services produced.
　　a. Economic growth　　　　　　　　　b. A Random Walk Down Wall Street
　　c. ABN Amro　　　　　　　　　　　　　d. AAB

57. _____ in finance is a risk management technique, related to hedging, that mixes a wide variety of investments within a portfolio. Because the fluctuations of a single security have less impact on a diverse portfolio, _____ minimizes the risk from any one investment.

A simple example of _____ is the following: On a particular island the entire economy consists of two companies: one that sells umbrellas and another that sells sunscreen.

　　a. 4-4-5 Calendar　　　　　　　　　　b. 7-Eleven
　　c. 529 plan　　　　　　　　　　　　　d. Diversification

58. In economics and related disciplines, a _____ is a cost incurred in making an economic exchange. For example, most people, when buying or selling a stock, must pay a commission to their broker; that commission is a _____ of doing the stock deal. Or consider buying a banana from a store; to purchase the banana, your costs will be not only the price of the banana itself, but also the energy and effort it requires to find out which of the various banana products you prefer, where to get them and at what price, the cost of traveling from your house to the store and back, the time waiting in line, and the effort of the paying itself; the costs above and beyond the cost of the banana are the _____s.

    a. Marginal cost
    b. Fixed costs
    c. Variable costs
    d. Transaction cost

ANSWER KEY

Chapter 1

1. b	2. a	3. c	4. d	5. d	6. d	7. d	8. b	9. a	10. c
11. d	12. d	13. d	14. d	15. b	16. b	17. d	18. b	19. c	20. a
21. b	22. d	23. c	24. a	25. d	26. c	27. b	28. d	29. c	30. d
31. d	32. d	33. a	34. d	35. d	36. a	37. d	38. d	39. d	

Chapter 2

1. b	2. d	3. d	4. d	5. d	6. d	7. c	8. d	9. b	10. a
11. b	12. d	13. d	14. a	15. d	16. d	17. a	18. d	19. d	20. a
21. d	22. b	23. c	24. d	25. a	26. b	27. d	28. a	29. d	30. a
31. a	32. a	33. d	34. d	35. d	36. d	37. b	38. b	39. d	40. b
41. d	42. a	43. b	44. a	45. d	46. c	47. d	48. d	49. c	50. a
51. d	52. d	53. b							

Chapter 3

1. c	2. a	3. d	4. b	5. d	6. d	7. a	8. d	9. d	10. d
11. d	12. b	13. d	14. d	15. a	16. b	17. d	18. d	19. b	20. d
21. d	22. d	23. d	24. d	25. b	26. d	27. d	28. b	29. d	30. d
31. c	32. a	33. d	34. d	35. d	36. c				

Chapter 4

1. b	2. d	3. d	4. c	5. d	6. d	7. b	8. d	9. b	10. d
11. d	12. a	13. c	14. d	15. c	16. d	17. d	18. d	19. d	20. d
21. b	22. b	23. a	24. c	25. a	26. d	27. a	28. d	29. a	30. d
31. b									

Chapter 5

| 1. c | 2. b | 3. b | 4. a | 5. a | 6. b | 7. d | 8. b | 9. c | 10. d |
| 11. c | 12. d | 13. d | 14. b | 15. d | 16. b | | | | |

Chapter 6

1. c	2. b	3. a	4. c	5. d	6. b	7. d	8. d	9. c	10. b
11. d	12. a	13. d	14. d	15. d	16. b	17. a	18. a	19. c	20. b
21. d	22. c	23. a	24. c	25. b	26. b	27. d	28. d	29. d	30. d
31. d	32. b	33. c	34. c	35. c	36. b	37. d	38. d	39. d	40. d
41. d	42. c	43. d	44. a	45. d	46. c	47. d			

Chapter 7

1. a	2. d	3. b	4. c	5. c	6. c	7. a	8. d	9. d	10. d
11. d	12. d	13. d	14. b	15. a	16. d	17. c	18. d	19. a	20. b
21. d	22. d	23. d	24. d	25. d	26. b	27. d	28. d	29. d	30. b
31. d	32. c								

Chapter 8
1. d	2. d	3. d	4. c	5. d	6. d	7. c	8. d	9. a	10. c
11. c	12. d	13. d	14. d	15. d	16. b	17. a	18. d	19. c	20. d
21. b	22. d	23. c	24. b	25. d	26. c	27. b			

Chapter 9
1. d	2. d	3. c	4. d	5. c	6. d	7. b	8. c	9. b	10. c
11. c	12. b	13. d	14. d	15. a	16. d	17. d	18. d	19. a	20. d
21. d	22. d	23. b	24. b	25. d	26. d	27. c	28. d	29. d	30. c
31. d	32. b	33. d	34. c	35. d	36. c	37. b			

Chapter 10
1. d	2. b	3. c	4. b	5. b	6. a	7. b	8. c	9. c	10. d
11. d	12. d	13. a	14. a	15. d	16. d	17. c	18. b	19. d	20. d
21. d	22. a	23. a	24. d	25. b	26. a	27. d	28. c	29. b	30. d
31. b	32. c	33. b	34. a	35. d					

Chapter 11
1. c	2. a	3. c	4. d	5. b	6. d	7. b	8. c	9. c	10. b
11. b	12. c	13. c	14. a	15. b	16. d	17. d	18. d	19. d	20. c
21. b	22. d	23. a	24. d	25. b	26. d	27. d	28. d	29. d	30. d

Chapter 12
1. c	2. b	3. b	4. d	5. d	6. d	7. d	8. d	9. d	10. d
11. c	12. d	13. b	14. d	15. d	16. b	17. d	18. d	19. d	20. d
21. d	22. a	23. a	24. d	25. d	26. d	27. d	28. d	29. d	30. d
31. b	32. d	33. d	34. d	35. a	36. a	37. d	38. b	39. d	

Chapter 13
1. d	2. d	3. b	4. d	5. b	6. a	7. d	8. d	9. d	10. a
11. d	12. d	13. d	14. d	15. d	16. d	17. d	18. d	19. d	20. d
21. d	22. d	23. d	24. d						

Chapter 14
1. d	2. c	3. d	4. a	5. b	6. d	7. b	8. d	9. d	10. c
11. d	12. b	13. a	14. d	15. d	16. d	17. c	18. d	19. d	20. d
21. d	22. d	23. a	24. d	25. b	26. d	27. b	28. a	29. d	30. d
31. d	32. d	33. d	34. a	35. c	36. d	37. d	38. d	39. d	40. d
41. d	42. d	43. a	44. c	45. b	46. d	47. b	48. d	49. d	50. d
51. b	52. b	53. d	54. d	55. d					

Chapter 15

1. d	2. d	3. b	4. b	5. a	6. d	7. b	8. d	9. b	10. d
11. b	12. d	13. a	14. a	15. d	16. d	17. d	18. c	19. c	20. c
21. b	22. d	23. d	24. d	25. c	26. b	27. b	28. d	29. d	30. d
31. b	32. b	33. d	34. c	35. c	36. d	37. d	38. d	39. b	40. d
41. d	42. d	43. d	44. d	45. b	46. a	47. d	48. a	49. c	50. d
51. d	52. b	53. b	54. b	55. a	56. a	57. d	58. d		